HIGH-TECH ETIQUETTE

PERFECTING THE ART OF PLUGGED-IN POLITENESS

Viva Books

New Delhi | Mumbai | Chennai | Kolkata | Bangalore | Hyderabad | Kochi

First Indian Edition 2004
Reprinted 2008

VIVA BOOKS PRIVATE LIMITED

- 4737/23 Ansari Road, Daryaganj, New Delhi 110 002
  E-mail: vivadelhi@vivagroupindia.net, Tel. 42242200
- Plot No. 76, Service Industries, Shirvane, Sector 1, Nerul, Navi Mumbai 400 706
  E-mail: vivamumbai@vivagroupindia.net, Tel. 27721273, 27721274
- Jamals Fazal Chambers, 26 Greams Road, Chennai 600 006
  E-mail: vivachennai@vivagroupindia.net, Tel. 28290304, 28294241
- B-103, Jindal Towers, 21/1A/3 Darga Road, Kolkata 700 017
  E-mail: vivakolkata@vivagroupindia.net, Tel. 22836381, 22816713
- 7, Sovereign Park Apartments, 56-58, K. R. Road, Basavanagudi, Bangalore 560 004
  E-mail: vivabangalore@vivagroupindia.net, Tel. 26607409, 26607410
- 101-102 Mughal Marc Apartments, 3-4-637 to 641, Narayanguda, Hyderabad 500 029
  E-mail: vivahyderabad@vivagroupindia.net, Tel. 27564481, 27564482
- First Floor, Beevi Towers, SRM Road, Kaloor, Kochi 682 018, Kerala
  E-mail: vivakochi@vivagroupindia.net, Tel: 0484-2403055, 2403056

Published by arrangement with

Rawdon and Watson Publishing Company
5930-E Royal Lane, PMB #221
Dallas, Texas 75230
USA

ISBN-10: 81-7649-613-8
ISBN-13: 978-81-7649-613-1

Published by Vinod Vasishtha for Viva Books Private Limited, 4737/23, Ansari Road, New Delhi 110 002. Printed and bound by Raj Press, R-3, Inderpuri, New Delhi - 110 012.

Dedication

It is with great love and gratitude that I dedicate this book to my loving husband, "the man of my dreams" Lee, who is my constant inspiration, who continues to believe in me, encourages me, and inspires me to be the best that I can be no matter how many times I lose my way. He has worked side by side with me throughout the entire process of writing and rewriting this book. He believed in me when I didn't believe in myself. He insisted I finish it even when I thought I couldn't. Without his unwavering love and devotion, this book would still be sitting on my computer. I could never thank him enough for the unconditional love that he has always given to me.

Acknowledgments

In writing a book, I have found that it doesn't take just one person. It isn't the author alone that writes a book. It is all of the dedicated people behind the book and the author that makes it happen.

First, I want to give a standing ovation to my husband who constantly worked hand in hand with me to complete my work. He offered advice, edited, corrected and added his great stories. I will always be thankful that God chose to introduce him to me! Lee, you are the love of my life.

Second, I want to acknowledge my daughters, Julie and Lorie, who also encouraged me and insisted that I finish what I started. Lorie's humor and "well-delivered" lines helped to set the tone for the book. Lorie spent hours helping with the editing before I sent it to the final editor and she always offered great ideas, her special wit and encouragement.

Julie never lost faith in me and kept telling me that wherever she was speaking, people were screaming for this book. She helped me to realize the great need for this type of book.

Julie and Lorie have been my best friends through thick and thin. Julie and Lorie are two beautiful, talented, creative, loving, intelligent ladies that I am so proud to call my daughters.

To my sons, Terry, Matthew and Jason, who are so much like Lee that when I was lucky enough to "step-in" to being their mother, my happiness increased just that much more! You are three wonderful men and I am so blessed to be able to share in your lives.

To my son, Jeff, I will always love you.

There have been so many wonderful friends who have encouraged and believed me from the start of my professional speaking business and authorship. Henry Gentry, Terry Seefluth, Maco Amoyo, Jim Sundelius, Dr. Jacque Lytle, Sharon Blewitt, Linda McGinnis, Ron Miller, Jodie Wallace, Lorri Allen, Princesses Sandy and Caryl, Hal, Ann and Read Davis and so many more that I cannot possibly name them all. You know who you are—you know how much you mean to me!

To my dearly beloved guardian angel, Grandma Hains, who loved me and encouraged me as a youth. She was my religious inspiration and mentor who showed me how important it is to turn to God in times of trouble and triumph. She believed in me and she set the example that has led me through life. She set this example for her precious daughter and my Aunt Norma who avidly carries the importance of the family spirit that Grandma did. So, to my Aunt Norma, not only have you continued to be an inspiration to your own children, you are an inspiration to me as well.

I could not forget the love and support of my Uncle Bill and Aunt Margie who have always encouraged me and also believed in me. The love you show for your family is an inspiration to all.

In memory of my father, who showed me strength through adversity, honesty, and gave me the entrepreneurial spirit.

I also must thank David Dunn of Jenkins Group as he worked closely with Lee and me through this project to make it become a reality.

To each of you named and unnamed, my deepest gratitude and thanks goes to you from the bottom of my heart.

With love and gratitude,
Jana

Contents

Introduction

"Life is not so short but that there is always time enough for courtesy."

—RALPH WALDO EMERSON (1803–1882)

AMOF :X the days of 7:-) good-bye! It is TEOTWAWKI. (Interpretation: *As a matter of fact, kiss the days of Fred Flintstone good-bye! It is The End Of The World As We Know It.)* Acronyms (Emoticons) have taken over the world (or the World Wide Web) and we must now learn this new language or retire with Fred Flintstone. Hundreds of Websites have been developed to inform the public on the latest invention of Emoticons. And still, the fact remains that whether in telecommunications or face-to-face meetings, the impression you make FIRST will be the impression that LASTS.

When you communicate with others on the Internet, they can't see or hear you. It is, therefore, even more crucial to take the time necessary to make sure your writing is clear, succinct and grammatically correct. Your writing style becomes your "body language" and you should be aware that information in writing tends to have more impact than verbal communication. The bad news seems worse and the good news seems better.

No more are we burdened with "snail mail." Electronic communication is fast, easy, inexpensive and effective. However, because it is both informal and one-sided, there are some potential disadvantages. E-mail *feels* casual and lacks the nuance or personality that is normally conveyed by voice inflections and body language. That means that e-mail has the potential of creating miscommunication that may be difficult to undo once you hit the "send" button.

E-mail messaging demonstrates your communication skills, knowledge, education and professionalism more clearly than ever before. Additionally, it can create a record that can be referred to by the people making decisions regarding your future. *The New York Times* fired 23 employees at an administrative center in Norfolk, VA for sending "inappropriate and offensive" e-mail messages (*The Dallas Morning News, Dec. 1, 1999*). E-mail must be used properly in business and at home.

And then there is Cell Yell, Voice Mail Jail, and traveling with communication devices. As the world becomes more closely connected with the inventions of telecommunication devices, we need to pay more attention to our manners and sharpen our protocol skills even more.

The impact of equipment snafus in business can be significant. Would you continue to do business with someone who treated you rudely by not returning your calls?

Repeatedly, research has shown that communication skills are THE most essential ingredients to success at home and in the office. Over 80% of marriages fail today and the reason most often cited is the lack of communication.

Wouldn't it be wonderful if someone would invent the "Manners Microchip?" This silicon device would automatically program our communication equipment for gracious and courteous operation. However, the problem with manners does not lie with the equipment, but with the people who use it.

What image do you project when you write your e-mails, send your faxes, record your voice mail or leave your messages? Do you think before you speak . . . or . . . write? Have you learned what is appropriate and will your message articulate the image you want?

The vast changes in electronic communication have highly impacted our fast-paced, global, and culturally diverse world.

Additionally, electronic communication has greatly increased both our ability to keep in touch and the speed with which we can share information. However, have we kept up with the protocol when using these devices?

If you are annoyed by cell phones ringing in meetings, theaters, church and other inappropriate places; if you are concerned with junk, long-winded, or even offensive e-mail; if you are put off by long, cutesy voice mail or swimming through the abyss of phone trees that waste your time, this book is for you. It begins where other etiquette books have left off. Being plugged-in or wireless is no excuse for being rude or inconsiderate. In fact, because many of these devices are portable and often used in public, we need to be even more careful than before to be considerate of people around us.

This book is intended to provide you with the most essential rules of protocol for electronic communication in an easy to read format, with a little touch of humor here and there! It is the authority of practical and powerful advice. It achieves the essential balance by giving you complete up-to-date and insightful information that can immediately be put to use without being burdened with complex details that you don't want, need, or have time for today.

Enjoy!

Chapter 1

Introduction to E-Mail Etiquette

You've Got Mail

A mother was teaching her three-year-old daughter the Lord's Prayer. Every evening at bedtime she repeated it after her mother. Finally the night came when Linda said she was ready to solo. The mother listened with pride as she carefully enunciated each word, right up to the end of the prayer . . . "Lead us not into temptation," she prayed, "but deliver us some e-mail. Amen."

Children today do not remember a time without e-mail. No matter what industry you work in, no matter what your position in the organization and no matter whether you own your own company, communication has changed and we must update our skills to coincide with the times.

Consider these changes seen by the 40+ Generation: (If you are over 40, you're going to love this!)

:-) If you are over 40, you were born before color television, penicillin, polio shots, frozen foods, Xerox, contact lenses, frisbees and the PILL!

:-) You were born before radar, credit cards, split atoms, laser beams and ballpoint pens; before panty hose, dishwashers, clothes dryers, electric blankets, air conditioners, drip-dry clothes and before man walked on the moon.

:-) You never heard of FM radio, tape decks, electric typewriters, artificial hearts, word processors, yogurt and guys wearing earrings.

:-) A "chip" meant a piece of wood; hardware meant hardware, and software wasn't even a word!

:-) Pizzas, "McDonald's" and instant coffee were unheard of.

:-) You could buy ice cream cones for a nickel or a dime.

:-) For one nickel, you could make a phone call, buy a Pepsi or ride a streetcar, or buy enough stamps to mail one letter and two postcards.

:-) You could buy a Chevy Coupe for $600 . . . but who could afford one? A pity too, because gas was 11 cents a gallon.

:-) COKE was a cold drink.

:-) POT was something you cooked in.

:-) ROCK MUSIC was a grandmother's lullaby.

:-) AIDS were helpers in the Principal's office.

And you would have been the last generation that was so dumb as to think you needed a husband to have a baby!

As you can clearly see, things are changing and so must we if we want to not just keep up or get ahead, but if we want to survive!

In 1594, Shakespeare wrote in his masterpiece, *Taming of the Shrew,* "We must frame our manners to the time." It is time that we learn the proper e-mail etiquette rules.

"Netiquette" or e-mail etiquette is the personal protocol that enables us be a part of a networked society. Most of all, we must remember that when we communicate via e-mail that we are still talking through the art of written communication, which used to be limited to letter writing. We are seen through the eyes of our written message and that is the only "body language" our readers will know. Courtesy and politeness extends to e-mail just as it does in our daily face-to-face communications.

"E-mail has been a blessing to me. I love the convenience of it. Because I have a home-based business in addition to a corporate, day-time job, I am able to keep up with clients by E-mailing after hours and on weekends and they can respond anytime they wish. On a more personal note, I love corresponding with friends who will E-mail, but would never write a letter. I have been in touch with high school teachers, friends and relatives that may have been lost to me forever, if not for this technology."

—Lorri Allen, Good News!

Most companies have gone to high-tech communications and are conducting business more through e-mail today than any other form of communication. It is convenient, easy to use and it helps us to conduct business more globally than ever before. We are not restricted by exorbitant long distance calling rates and time zones. We can send an e-mail to almost anywhere in the world at any hour and receive an answer within 24 hours.

Intel employees worldwide receive an average of 3 million E-mails a day. The average Intel employee spends 2 ½ hours each day dealing with these messages.

—*American Way*, 6/15/01

Many standard business documents are frequently transmitted via e-mail, including résumés, memos, meeting agendas, proposals, contracts, brochures, news or research articles and newsletters.

With this in mind, it is necessary to make sure that we use the correct punctuation, grammar and spelling in every communication we use. Many books have been written regarding wedding, business and social protocol over the years, but new etiquette dictates that we sharpen our manners once again with the new telecommunication rules.

Many of our original etiquette rules come from England and France who set the standard for the rest of the world as it developed. Today, however, the United States is one of the leaders in electronic development and with that comes the responsibility of setting the standard for electronic courtesies.

Etiquette means "ticket" or "label" in French. When using the Internet, we are using the electronic "ticket" to travel first class from our home or office without the annoying crowds, lines and costs of traveling first class. Nevertheless, we must remember that we are still in public and the rules of courtesy will "label" us. That first impression will always remain the lasting impression.

Take the time necessary to make your writing clear and succinct as possible. Utilize the available tools, such as spell check and grammar check programs before you send your e-mail messages. However, even if you do use a spell check program, always proofread the message *before* you hit the send button.

Maybe you have heard of the infamous "Wicked Bible." In 1631, King Charles I ordered 1,000 Bibles from an English printer named Robert Barker. Only after the Bibles were delivered did anyone notice a serious mistake: The word "not" had been left out of the Seventh Commandment! "Thou shall [not] commit adultery." *Exodus 20:14*

Charles was not amused by the "Wicked Bible," as the infamous printing mistake was called. He ordered the Bibles recalled and destroyed, took away Barker's license to print Bibles and fined him 300 Pounds, which was a large sum of money in those days. With this one *little* mistake, Barber found himself out of business.

Remember that "Spell Check" will not flag an error if you use the wrong word correctly spelled, i.e. "We are *no* interested in your proposal" when you mean "We are *not* interested in your proposal." These typographical errors make your message (and you) appear sloppy and unprofessional, but at least the reader can figure out what you mean.

However, imagine the confusion and possible damage if you make another common typographical error and leave out a word . . . "We are interested in your proposal." These errors can only be prevented by careful proofreading. Spell check is an aid, not a miracle cure.

Amy Vanderbilt once wrote, *"There is nothing more pleasant than receiving a beautiful letter."* Sometimes a letter sent by mail or a phone call is more appropriate than sending an e-mail. *People Magazine* reported in their August 2000 issue of an instance where "someone recently e-mailed [me] the news that a member of [my] family had died." That is outrageous! Who could be so cold or insensitive that a personal phone call was not made to report such sad news? Have we become so busy that we don't have time to show common courtesies? This has to be one of the worst faux pas I have ever read regarding e-mail etiquette.

Whether you are corresponding by postal mail or e-mail, there are certain written conventions that will give your words polish and class and make no mistake, e-mail is written correspondence and is no different than mail sent by the conventional method. Therefore, it is just as important that you apply a few simple techniques and invest a little extra effort in polishing your manners to give you a competitive edge and leave a favorable impression.

Chapter 2

The Basics of E-Mail Etiquette

Putting It in Writing

Many years ago when an ice cream sundae cost much less than today, a little boy named Jeffery went into an ice cream parlor and sat at the counter. The waitress put a glass of water in front of him as the little boy asked, "How much is an ice cream sundae?" "Fifty cents," the waitress replied.

The little boy pulled his hand out of his pocket and counted the number of coins in it. "How much is a dish of plain vanilla?" he asked. Some other people were waiting to order and the waitress became impatient. "Thirty-five cents," she said angrily.

Jeffery counted his coins again. "Ok," he said, "I'll have the plain vanilla ice cream."

The waitress brought the ice cream and walked away. The little boy finished, paid the cashier, and departed. When the waitress came back, she swallowed hard at what she saw. There, placed neatly beside the empty dish, were two nickels and five pennies—her tip.

Wouldn't it be nice if everyone we met were this thoughtful? It's really a matter of just being patient and taking some time for courtesies.

In the writing of e-mail messages, things have not really changed with the proper way to set up a message. Let's review the basic rules of writing your correspondence on the Internet.

Greetings and Salutations

There is no doubt that as the world becomes more global, we seem to become less formal. However, when you write a letter, call someone on the phone or see someone in person, do you just launch into a conversation or do you show common courtesy by greeting him or her? Of course, you say, "Hello" or "Dear Sir." So why is it that so many people begin their e-mail messages without the proper salutation? Use the same salutation and punctuation that you would as if you are writing a letter. Use a colon for the formal salutation and a comma for the informal greeting. *(e.g. Dear Ms. Smith: Dear Sue,)*

One of the most common mistakes in correspondence is beginning the first sentence of the message with the word "I." E-mail etiquette dictates that you do not begin your message with the word "I" as well.

Closing With Courtesy

The complimentary closing in an e-mail message can be kept brief by writing just your name. Unlike formal or personal correspondence, it is not necessary to write "Sincerely yours" or "Yours truly." However, it is completely correct to establish an individual electronic "signature" closing. Since e-mails are not on official company letterhead, I have created my own electronic signature by using "SMILE FOR SUCCESS" and include my full name and all other relevant contact information. One of my clients uses the company's vision statement as her electronic signature. This can be done if it is professional and displays good taste. In replying to a client or business associate it is important to include your pertinent information just under your signature at the end of the message.

The Senate unanimously passed a bill June 16, 2000 allowing consumers and businesses to sign contracts online with a click of a mouse. The measure easily cleared the House on June 14, 2000 and went into effect on October 1, 2000.

Signatures have entered the digital age. A digital signature is not an electronic image of a handwritten signature, but rather, it is an algorithm made up of ones and zeros, one unique to each transaction, activated by the purchaser's electronic key. I know this sounds confusing, but it's really not.

It is much like a social security number, driver's license number, or an ATM PIN number. The idea is to become a paperless society. And, I guess the "up-side" of the new electronic signature is that those with bad handwriting won't have to make excuses anymore why they have poor penmanship.

It's simple to bank online, get a mortgage, or buy tickets to the local movie theater. We can order flowers, gifts and go "garage sale" hunting by bidding on everything from model trains to out of print Elvis movies! However, every time we enter our personal information, there is a risk of a hacker finding a way to duplicate our e-signature. It is because of this problem that many people are very leery of shopping, paying bills or applying for credit on line.

By giving electronic signatures the legal weight of paper signatures, the new law gives consumers the opportunity to buy health insurance, complete bank loans or set up brokerage accounts over the Internet, around the clock and with no delay. It is imperative to be cautious when conducting such important financial business over the Internet this way as you are opening yourself up to the possibility of hackers and other abuse. Although the idea of being able to "speed-up" the process of such business with an electronic signature, the bill has a lack of technical specifications that leave poorly constructed electronic transactions open to fraud.

USA TODAY, August 23, 2000 reports that online bill-payment service Paytrust said that it would acquire competitor PayMyBills.com in a bid to solidify its foothold in this fast-growing market. The services enable consumers to receive, review and pay bills online. Paytrust and PayMyBills provide the payment technology and service to companies and in return, these companies pay different fees.

We can order food and services and most anything we want over the Internet, pay bills, and sign contracts. Be careful what you order and sign for on the Internet.

Be Specific With The Subject Line

The subject line is the way that most people "screen" their e-mail. It is the equivalent of retrieving your voice mail messages or reading the pieces of mail that are most appealing to you first. Therefore, be descriptive if you want your message read in a timely manner. Avoid crying, "wolf." If you constantly write "URGENT!" on the subject line, readers will grow weary of what is really urgent (to them).

Sometimes the Subject Line can be too specific. A woman sent a baby shower notice to her friends with the Subject Line reading "Lunch and a Shower." Her husband, who was sent a "Copy to" message, replied that he was disappointed when he saw that he wasn't the only recipient.

—*READERS DIGEST*

Think Before You Write!

Didn't your mother always tell you to "Think before you Speak"? In the case of e-mail, it applies in the sense of thinking before you write your message. Your postings reflect on you. Most people will know you only by what you say and how well you say it. In the case of e-mail, they will know you by what you write and how well you write it. If you are upset or angry, wait to respond. Take time to phrase your thoughts in a clear and concise manner. Also, remember that the Internet (and cell phones) is less private than other forms of communication. Your message may be accidentally (or intentionally) sent to a large audience. In fact, thousands of people may read your message. Information posted on the Net can come back to haunt you or the person you are talking about. Think twice before you write personal information or talk about someone else.

Observe the Golden Rule and Practice the Platinum Rule

Tried and true, the Golden Rule has always been a great premise for treating people. However, Dr. Tony Alessandra created the Platinum Rule, which takes the Golden Rule to a new level. He says, "Do unto Others as *They* Would Like Done unto *Them*." This concept takes into consideration something the Golden Rule does not. It points out that there are certain ways that people want to be treated and it is not necessarily the way you want to be treated. You may like forwards, jokes, and stories, but many business people do not have the time or the desire to read such e-mail.

USA Today (August 23, 2000) reported that Dow Chemical was planning to fire 40 employees and discipline several others at a Texas plant after a review of 6,000 e-mail accounts turned up pornography and violent subject matter. If you have been unwittingly added to a forward or mailing list that engages in this type of e-mail, be aware of the consequences. E-mail is public and traceable.

Be Careful with Humor and Sarcasm

Without the voice inflections and body language of personal communication, it is easy to misinterpret remarks meant to be funny. Subtle humor tends to get lost. Take steps to make sure people realize that you are trying to be funny. Use an emoticon such as a smiley face **:-)** or **:-D**. However, no matter how broad the humor or satire, it is safer to remind people that you are joking. But also be aware that frequently satire is posted without explicit indications.

If you are the recipient of something that offends you, you do have the right to let the sender know your feelings. I received an e-card that I found to be very offensive and I wrote back to the sender, "I opened your Christmas card and was disappointed to see that it was risqué. I was surprised that you would send something like that to me. I don't really like that kind of humor."

The sender replied right away with an apology and said that she agreed that it was inappropriate and thanked me for pointing out her faux pas.

Check Your E-Mail Often

Just as you should check your telephone messages at least once a day, you should also check your e-mail messages often. Remember that people who send e-mails are usually looking for a quick response. Business deals are made or lost in seconds. I have always made it my practice to call for messages when I am on the road at 10 a.m., 12, 2, and 4 p.m. and check my e-mail messages at 12 and 4 p.m. Establish your schedule and let your office know what they can count on in your absence.

Respond in a Timely Fashion

E-mail is considered to be the fastest form of communication today and no one ever likes being "put on hold." Try to make it your practice to respond to your messages within 24 hours. If you are going to be out of the office for a long period of time, whether working or on vacation, provide for an "automatic reply" if your program is capable of doing so. This is a message that automatically acknowledges the receipt of the message and responds to the sender with the information about when you will return.

In your replies, you should include enough of the original message to provide a context. Remember that Electronic Mail is not as immediate as a telephone conversation and the recipient may not recall the contents of the original message, especially if he or she receives many messages each day. Including the relevant section from the original message helps the recipient to place your reply in context. Include only the minimum you need from the original message. One of the most annoying things you can encounter in e-mail is to have your original five page message quoted back at you in its entirety, with the words "Me too" added at the bottom. Quote back only the smallest amount you need to make your context clear.

Use some kind of visual indication to distinguish between text quoted from the original message and your new text—this makes the reply much easier to follow. The symbol ">" is a traditional marker for quoted text, but you can use anything provided its purpose is clear and you use it consistently.

Pay careful attention to where your reply is going to end up; it can be embarrassing for you if a personal message ends up on a mailing list, and it's generally annoying for the other members on the list.

Ask yourself if your reply is really warranted—a message sent to a list server which only says "I agree" is probably better sent privately to the person who originally sent the message.

Supply Sufficient Information

I have often been contacted via e-mail with a message to "call me," but the sender neglects to send their phone number. This has happened for years when people leave phone messages instructing me to return their call, but do not leave their number. When I am traveling, I do not carry my entire Address Book and if the caller is not courteous enough to leave their number (slowly), I cannot return the call.

I recently received an 'urgent' e-mail message to call the sender that day as they had to make a decision by the end of the day for a speaking engagement that I was very interested in presenting. However, the sender did not supply his number and I had no idea which company it was for. I could only respond to the e-mail, which was not picked up until two days later. An apology was given, but he hired another speaker. This situation is frustrating and is a common occurrence in business. If you want to communicate on the phone after the e-mail message, be sure to send your number. It's always a good idea to include your signature at the end of you messages that gives your name, phone number, company, e-mail address and website if you have one.

Chapter 3

Common E-Mail Faux Pas to Avoid

It's All in the Delivery!

Why is it that $10 looks so small at the grocery store, but so big at church?

A one-dollar bill and a one-hundred dollar bill got folded together one day and began talking about their life experiences.

The one-hundred dollar bill began to brag: "I've had a great life," he said. "I have been in all the big hotels. I have been in casinos and in the wallets of some of the most important executives. I have flown from one end of the country to the other."

In awe, the dollar bill responded humbly, "Gee, nothing like that has ever happened to me . . . but I have been to church a lot."

It's all in the delivery and perception is everything. Others evaluate our worth in many ways, but I assure you that the way we communicate, whether verbal or written, will determine the perception of our intelligence, knowledge, experience and education level. Make your "deliveries" with confidence by avoiding these common e-mail faux pas.

Proofread Your Messages

There are many things to look for when you proofread your message *before* you send it. Make sure it reads the way you want it to read and that you use the correct language for the meaning of the sentence. Many words in the English language are pronounced the same, but have entirely different meanings. For example, "threw" is the past tense verb for throw. Whereas "through" can be an adjective, adverb or preposition, all having a slightly different meaning. I have found the most common misuse of similar words are "to," "too," and "two." "Two" is the cardinal number between one and three. "To" means direction, and "too" is another word for also. The bottom line is simple. Take the time to read your work *before* you post it. The reader will form an instant impression from your posting, just as they do when they read correspondence received through conventional mail.

Additionally, it is easy to type the wrong word, such as "you" instead of "your" or "though" instead of "thought." Recently I received a message from a top executive of a Fortune 500 company beginning with "though you would enjoy . . . ." Obviously, "though" should have been "thought." "Though" was the incorrect word and wasn't even capitalized although it was the beginning of the sentence and the first word in the e-mail. I was not impressed.

Don't Burn Yourself With Spelling Flames and Resist the Urge to Correct!

Spelling mistakes can be disastrous. Use spell check before you send your messages.

If you receive a message with typos or misspellings, resist the urge to correct the sender. This is not usually well received unless you are the sender's grammar professor. It is not your job to correct others' postings. This will only cause anger and resentment. Further, many people suffer from dyslexia and have difficulty noticing their spelling mistakes and some "Netizens" use English as a second language and get confused. If you feel that you must make a comment, do so by mail, on the phone, or in person.

Always remember that there is a difference between etiquette and manners. Etiquette is defined as the rules, the protocol and the formalities. Manners are the courtesies, politeness and refinement. You may know the rules, but you should choose wisely and carefully in imposing your knowledge of the rules on others. Often it is much better to resist the temptation of unnecessarily correcting people.

Miss Manners, Judith Martin, was asked by one of her readers what advice would she give regarding a distant relative who sent e-mails typed in all uppercase and also misspelled her name in each letter. The reader stated that she politely e-mailed back to her relative pointing out the faux pas and explained that she was sure there was no malice on his part. The reader simply wanted to know if she had done the correct thing by pointing out the errors.

Ms. Martin replied that this is clearly the "complexity of etiquette." She wrote, "There is a rule against correcting others, but there is also a rule against allowing [people] to cause offensive unawares by leaving them ignorant of the rules. By obeying one, you disobey the other."

Ultimately, the call to correct or not correct is yours. However, if you are in doubt about how your corrections will be received—don't correct. At any rate, be careful and considerate in correcting others and only correct mistakes when actually necessary.

"In the early days of E-mail, when we didn't really know how to use it that well, my husband accidentally sent a scathing E-mail about my best friend to my best friend. It was the beginning of the end for that friendship. She thought he and I sent it intentionally and I did not even know she had received it. She didn't tell me until months later, and it became too late, in her eyes to repair the relationship. Some say accidents don't happen, but I still miss her friendship."

—Lorri Allen, Good News!

Critical Flames are Rude

There are two kinds of "flames" in the world of dot.com. We have already discussed spelling flames, but there are also critical flames. Strongly critical messages on the net are called "Flames." If you cannot face the person and say what you have on your mind, do not write it in e-mail. Nasty words written in haste create more problems than they can solve. Once written, you cannot take it back, but you can hit "delete" and never send it.

Grammar Gaffes Can Hurt Your Image

If you are not sure of the proper grammar, look it up. Consider your audience. Is this a formal, traditional or more relaxed communication? Keep a simple reference book at your fingertips to refer to often. I recommend Jan Venolia's book, *Write Right!* California: Ten Speed Press, 3rd Edition, Revised 1995.

Punctuation is Vitally Important In Your E-Mail Message

Using the proper punctuation can leave either a positive or negative impression on your reader. If you are not sure of the proper punctuation, find out before you send that message to a prospective employer, business associate or your future mother-in-law!

Keep Your E-Mail Messages Short and Simple

You've heard the expression, "KISS." The KISS Rule applies more than anything in e-mail etiquette. If you are sending more than a "screen's worth" of information, make it an attachment. The shorter your message, the more likely it will be read AND answered.

Brevity is bliss in your e-mail messages. If someone sends you a long e-mail, it's appropriate to acknowledge that you received it, even if you do not have time to return a long response. If you get a play-by-play account of a friend's vacation, you could simply reply, "Sounds like you had a wonderful time. Thanks for the update. Great to hear from you. Things are going well here. I am looking forward to seeing you soon."

Score With Your Spacing!

Many of the e-mails that I receive are improperly formatted. Everything runs together with no paragraphs or distinction between the salutation, body and the closing. Did we throw out the rules of correct spacing with e-mail messages? NO, PLEASE, NO! Let's practice a simple "two-4-two" rule.

1. After the salutation, enter TWO spaces.
2. In between the paragraphs, enter TWO spaces.
3. After the final sentence, enter TWO spaces.
4. After the closing, enter TWO spaces and then sign your name.

Don't Shout!

When you type your message in all capitals, it's known as "shouting" in the e-mail world and people will resent you yelling at them. An all capitalized message may offend some people. Occasionally you can use uppercase letters to highlight items when you are making a special point and want attention drawn to something. You can also set a word off with **asterisks** or <<brackets>>. However, use all caps sparingly. It is best to use upper and lower case letters, just as you would in a letter. Additionally, all uppercase text becomes tiresome and very difficult to read. All caps also eliminate the availability to show emphasis when you need it.

Chapter 4

Advanced E-Mail Considerations

In London, Claire and Brad had a passionate date. The next morning Claire sent Brad an e-mail thanking him for a great evening and included a few private comments about his "studliness." This turned out to be a big mistake. Not being able to resist bragging, Brad forwarded the e-mail to several of his friends. Of course, this was just too good to keep to themselves, so they passed it on to a few of their friends.

Within a week, this message, amended with Brad's personal note boasting of his sexual manhood, had been e-mailed throughout London and worldwide. Since Claire and Brad included their complete names, the media picked up this story and started following them for the newest version of a Monica Lewinsky story, British style! To Claire's horror, she couldn't go anywhere without the media following her!

Claire worked for a dot.com company and sent the message from her office to Brad's office, which created another problem for the hot couple. Both of their companies are reviewing if they should be fired for using "company resources" for personal use. Brad's law firm has a clear company policy that specifically prohibits the sending and receipt of non-work-related material; in particular, obscene, discriminatory or defamatory material and junk mail.

At this writing, no decision had been made regarding either person's future with their companies.

Of course, the moral to this story is not to put anything in print that you don't want your mother or the media to read! E-mails are being forwarded everyday and the damage they can cause is much like that of Claire's message. She ended up in hiding and dashing from house to house with the British media hot on her trail.

Lawyers are predicting a glut of "cybersmear" libel lawsuits by targets of malicious online gossip. "Companies are not particularly sensitive about someone standing next to a water cooler and griping about someone else," says Blake Bell, a New York lawyer and editor of a Website called *CyberSecuritieslaw.com*, "But these messages go out to so many people that they're very concerned."

If you don't have something nice to say . . . don't say it, and for goodness sake, don't put it in writing. Candid conversation makes sense online, but use good judgment. An offhand remark behind someone's back is just one click away from being forwarded and landing on the front of that person's computer screen. Often this happens inadvertently when people respond to an e-mail and press the REPLY ALL button. The next thing you know, everyone knows exactly what you think of your boss or mother-in-law.

Before you press SEND, remember "The Digital Miranda" warning—"What you e-mail can be used against you."

Since few can resist e-mailing humorous forwarded jokes to friends, wouldn't it be nice to know they are not lingering in company files? The oil and gas giant, Chevron, would have been happy if that had been the case when an e-mail containing jokes such as "25 reasons beer is better than women" was used along with other evidence in a sexual-harassment claim. The company ended up settling the case for $2.2 million.

Professional and personal protocol dictates specific common sense rules in regards to all forms of communications, but particular discretion should be used in written e-mail correspondence.

Forwarding Faux Pas

If you are "one of those" Netizens who just has to forward every good joke, story, saying, poem and quote, I would suggest that you think twice, no, three times, before you hit "send." Busy people do not have the time to read all of this "stuff," and this is one way that viruses are spread. Wonderful people with good intentions unknowingly forward viruses. If a forward has an attachment, I will not open it. This is exactly how most viruses are spread.

If you are tempted to forward something or send a message that is just too juicy for words, consider enrolling yourself in THE E-MAIL FORWARDER'S 12 STEP PROGRAM. No membership fee and no dues, just say these words with me . . .

:-) I will NOT have bad luck, lose my friends, or delete my mailing lists if I don't forward an e-mail.

:-) I will NOT hear any music or see a taco dog if I do forward an e-mail.

:-) Bill Gates is NOT going to give me money and Victoria's Secret doesn't know anything about a gift certificate they are supposed to send to me.

:-) Ford will NOT give me a 50% discount on a new car, even if I forward my e-mail to more that 50 people.

:-) I will NEVER receive gift certificates, coupons, or freebies from Coca-Cola, Cracker Barrel, Old Navy, or anyone else by sending an e-mail to 25 people.

:-) I will NEVER see a pop up window if I forward an e-mail . . . NEVER . . . NEVER!!

:-) There is NO SUCH THING as an e-mail tracking program and I am NOT STUPID ENOUGH to think that someone will send me $100 for forwarding an e-mail to 10 or more people.

:-) There is NO kid in England with cancer collecting anything through the Make-a-Wish Foundation. Yes, he did have cancer when he was seven years old. Today he is 35 and cancer free and he doesn't want any more letters or get-well cards!

:-) The government DOES NOT have a bill in Congress called 901B (or whatever they named it this week) that, if passed, will enable them to charge us five cents for every e-mail we send.

:-) There will be NO cool dancing, singing, waving, colorful flowers, characters or special programs that I will receive immediately after I forward an e-mail. NONE, ZIP, ZERO, NADA!

:-) The American Red Cross will NOT donate 50 cents to a certain individual dying of some never-heard-of disease for every e-mail address I send this to. The American Red Cross doesn't MAKE donations—it RECEIVES them.

:-) And finally, I WILL NOT let others guilt me into sending things by telling me I am not their friend or that I don't believe in God or Jesus Christ. If God wants to send me a message, I believe the bushes in my yard will burn before He picks up a PC to deliver it!

Now, repeat this to yourself until you have memorized it and send it along to at least five of your friends before the next full moon or you will surely be ill for the next three months and all of your hair will fall out!

One last consideration in regard to forwarding e-mails comes from a former employee of a major corporation. She tells me that her former employer used an e-mail mailing list to notify an entire department of meetings, training, notices, etc. If recipients have questions, their replies would go to the entire list, so many times she would have to read 25 messages not intended for her. Firms can set up a system in which replies go only to the sender. If you are using your personal e-mail system at home, be careful when you hit the "reply" button and make sure that your reply is sent to the person it is intended for and not everybody on a mailing list.

SPAM—"The Other White Meat!"

Have you ever wondered what the canned meat product, SPAM, is really made from? I am told that the name was derived from "spices and ham." I have my own theory of the *real* contents of Spam. However, I think that considering the overall conception of "the other white meat" that the Professors of Internet Lingo have appropriately dubbed junk and unwanted e-mail Spam with good reason.

> **"Time is money and Spam is theft!"**
>
> —Rich Amato, Excel Communications

I once read this statement, "One person's junk is another's jewel." Chain letters and junk mail can add up. If you would prefer not to receive chain letters, it's appropriate to send a quick e-mail to the sender saying that while you love staying in touch, you would prefer not to receive chain letters. If you would like to curb unwanted "junk mail," look in your mail controls for some useful tricks on managing your incoming mail.

As a general rule, make sure the recipient would appreciate unsolicited e-mail. Keep in mind that although something may be of interest to you, it may not necessarily be of interest to the recipient. It is important to be considerate of the recipient's time and interest. If there is no value in your correspondence, the recipient may consider it "spamming" and hurt an otherwise good relationship.

"My biggest pet peeve with E-mail is spam sent from friends. We are all so busy, so the less time I waste cleaning out my inbox, the better. I wish that people would ask me before putting me on joke distribution lists, that nobody would send me chain letters, and that people would research bogus virus alerts before sending them. This is just plain learning how to respect the value of one's time."

—Kent Matthews, WebShop

Confidentiality Counts

Can't anyone keep a secret today? When I was a very young girl, my mother used to tell me to only write or say things that I wouldn't mind HER reading or hearing. Good advice then and it remains good advice today.

The FBI is investigating a Colorado woman who has been accused of trying to recruit a North Carolina man to kill her husband and make the incident look like an accident. In exchange, the hitman would receive half of her husband's $200,000 life insurance policy.

The woman and man met in a chat room on America Online, where she solicited his help. The man tipped off law enforcement authorities, then helped set up a meeting between an undercover FBI agent posing as his associate and the suspect.

The woman said she wanted her husband killed because of "past infidelities and his continued verbal and mental abuse," according to authorities.

PC does not always stand for "personal computer." You never know what can come back to haunt you. This was a tough lesson for more than 20 Northwest Airlines workers who were among those suspected of coordinating a sickout. In an effort to uncover incriminating e-mail, their home computers were seized for forensic evidence. Along with their e-mails, other personal records on their computers were examined.

Big Brother is watching! According to the American Management Association, 45% of U. S. businesses report they monitor employees' use of electronic communications, including e-mail. You can't be sure that yours isn't one of them.

Any interaction you have had with an individual via e-mail is copied and stored on multiple servers and can be subpoenaed at any time. While on her honeymoon, Catherine Davis sent several private e-mails to her friends back home. Unfortunately, that same laptop computer contained some deleted e-mails from her friend, Monica Lewinsky. After Special Prosecutor Ken Starr subpoenaed the laptop, both the Monica e-mails and the honeymoon correspondence were published and Catherine's husband, along with the rest of the world, found out that her honeymoon might have been premature.

Be careful what you write as it can easily get in the wrong hands. Likewise, be respectful by treating your electronic messages confidential and refrain from forwarding or sharing an e-mail message unless you have been given permission to do so by the sender.

Be an Attachment Ace

A large attachment will take a long time to download and will use more memory space. Anything more than one page should be faxed. Be careful with the graphics. Not everyone may have the super-fast computer and Internet connection that you do. I belong to an organization that enthusiastically hit "send" 142 times with an extensive e-mail message containing tons of graphics, which caused my entire computer to freeze. Not only was I unable to download a single file (each was over five megs in size and took too long to download), but 142 of these large files filled my mailbox and prevented any new messages from being received. Only after several phone calls and unbelievable aggravation was I able to restart my computer and restore my mail system, but many important files were lost forever. Be considerate before sending lengthy attachments.

The Vex of Viruses, Vigilante Viruses, and Urban Legends

Although most of us have virus scanners on our machines, they only scan for known viruses. Each time a new virus is created and spread, a new vaccine to cure it must be invented. Update your virus protection often to add these new cures. The best way to avoid viruses is never to open anything, especially attachments, from anyone you do not recognize even when the subject line is enticing.

Many large corporations have established procedures to minimize the danger of viruses. However, even with these intricate procedures many large corporations have suffered catastrophic data loses. Many small businesses and individuals cannot afford these expensive procedures and do not have virus protection or established procedures. Be cautious. Be careful. Be aware. Carelessness can cost you greatly!

Urban legends are somewhat entertaining the first time they come out; forgivable the second time, but the eighth time they hit and have been circulating for months or years, they become downright irritating.

Urban legends continue because there are always new users who haven't read them before and think they are new to everybody. Given all the Urban Legend and Virus Hoax information available all across the Web, it is a shame that users are willing to damage their own credibility by believing them.

> **"Even more annoying than junk E-mail and faxes are the arrogant spammers who try to justify their behavior by sending or forwarding urban legends."**
>
> —BOB CULMER, FULMINATA

Hoaxes bear the classic marks of an urban legend. There's no name, date or other facts to allow anyone to verify it. The Centers for Disease Control and Prevention deals with so many hoaxes daily, that they have set up a Website just for debunking them. (www.cdc.gov/hoax_rumors.htm)

My last thought on Vigilante Viruses and Urban Legends . . . if it isn't on the 6 o'clock news, it's probably not true. Hit "delete" and move on!

Cc (Copies) and Bcc (Blind Copies) Use and Abuse

Before copying everyone in your e-mail address book, decide if it is really necessary to send your message to everyone. It is bad manners to copy everyone and shows a lack of consideration and respect of people's time. Do not overuse your mailing list. Only send a message to people who need to receive it. By limiting your list of recipients, you will build your credibility as an e-mail virtuoso.

Also consider that some people would rather their e-mail address not be given to the general public. By sending copies to everyone on your mailing list, it opens up a door that some people would rather keep locked. We have the advantage of unlisted phone numbers and can screen our telephone calls with caller ID, but we cannot prevent other people from taking our e-mail addresses off of massive e-mail lists. If you are going to address a lengthy Cc list, it is best to put the addresses in the Bcc line so that others cannot read it. However, use the Bcc sparingly, because it may be interpreted that you are going behind someone's back by hiding the names of other recipients.

On the other hand, if you are sending mass interoffice e-mail and displaying the address list is not a problem, put the addresses in alphabetical order by the recipients' last name. Doing so keeps you from accidentally insulting people, such as your supervisor or manager because you listed them in the wrong place.

Return Receipt Requested

If you receive an e-mail message that is stamped with a receipt notification and you do not want to "officially" open it, just forward a copy of the message to yourself and read the copy.

What's Appropriate and What's Appalling??

Companies today are forced to write specific policies regarding what is appropriate e-mail. *The New York Times* fired 23 employees for 'inappropriate' e-mail. Times policy says that e-mail communication "must be consistent with conventional standards of ethical and proper conduct, behavior and manners are not to be used to create, forward or display any offensive or disruptive messages, including photographs, graphics and audio materials."

However, when someone in my seminar audience says that her boss uses e-mail in the office for everything from "I noticed you were late to work again" to "We are changing our Friday dress code." I believe we need to address the issue that bosses aren't exempt from what's appropriate and what is not! Management should not discipline their staff over e-mail for any reason, but sending out a general e-mail of a change in company policy is completely acceptable.

Don't send bad news over the Internet. Many employees today are being notified via e-mail of job layoffs, spending cuts, mergers and buyouts, that directly affect their lives and income.

Death Notices and Funeral Facts?

Notifying friends and family by e-mail of a death of a close friend, co-worker, or relative is just plain cold! If you don't have the time to call everyone that needs to know about the passing of someone, set up a phone tree to let people know the sad news.

Invitations on the Internet?? No!

Personal invitations to private functions should be sent through the mail or a personal phone call may be appropriate in some instances.

Business functions such as networking meetings, chambers of commerce events, or gatherings of a large number of the general organization or general public may be sent through e-mail. This saves organizations thousands of dollars in postage a year and is more efficient with the time of volunteers and employees. **BEWARE . . . .** Do not overload the invitation with graphics! Many programs are not equipped to open an extensive, overloaded, cutesy invitation. Be clear. Be concise.

E-Cards vs. Snail-Mail Cards??

More and more people in my seminars are complaining that they resent the thoughtlessness of an E-card, as it takes no effort to send them. I think that when you send E-cards just for fun and not for any special reason, they are appropriate and fun to get. However, on anniversaries, birthdays and special occasions, get off your derriere and go select a beautiful, thoughtful card and write a special message in it!

Thank-You Notes Appropriate?? No!

This is a great way to expedite a fast thank you to someone, but it will not replace the handwritten note of thanks. Think about when you get your mail. Don't you quickly browse through it, throwing the bills and advertisements to the side? Then you see the handwritten card and don't you always open that first? Of course, you do. It is always nice in the midst of the bills and junk mail to get a note of acknowledgment.

Consider this example. A manager helped an employee on a difficult project. The employee sent an electronic version of a thank-you note. The manager was not impressed. "I get a card that basically costs nothing and required no effort to send, after I gave so much. Am I supposed to be flattered by that?"

Take the time to write the note, using these protocol guidelines:

:-) Use nice stationery.

:-) Write in a timely manner. Although, later is better than not at all.

:-) Make a specific reference to the gift, meeting, lunch, and service.

:-) Use sincere and appreciative words.

:-) Explain how you are going to use the gift.

:-) Praise the item without lying even if you don't like it.

:-) Close with a personal sentiment.

:-) It is also appropriate to use a stamp rather than use a postage machine and never use a label or type a thank you note.

E-Mail Terms

A few e-mail terms your should familiarize yourself with are as follows:

Bandwidth. The information-carrying capacity of the wires and channels that connects everyone in cyberspace.

Bandwidth on Usernet. A measure of network capacity that is often wasted by people complaining about how items posted by others are a waste of bandwidth.

Bot. A piece of software that acts on behalf of and in place of a remote human (taken from the word *robot*).

Bounce. A message that was returned to the sender, either because the e-mail address was incorrect or because there was a denigration problem on the receiver's end. It can also be a verb: "I tried sending an e-mail to my Uncle Bill, but it bounced. I guess he doesn't work there any more."

Bozo Filter. also known as a 'kill file'. An option on some e-mail clients that automatically screens out e-mail from people whose messages you deem unworthy of reading.

Client. A computer system or process that requests a service of another computer system or process (a "server") using some kind of protocol and accepts the server's responses. A client is part of a client-server software architecture. E-mail software and a browser are both examples of a client.

Distribution List. A single e-mail address that resends to many others, allowing a discussion to continue easily among a quasi-stable group of participants. Also called e-mailing lists or Listservers (short for **list servers**).

Executable. A file containing a program that is ready to be executed.

Listbot. A piece of software that manages distribution lists. Also called a listserver or majordomo (after the name of a common list server).

Lurk. To read messages anonymously (in either a mailing list or Usenet newsgroup) without posting.

Mailbot. A piece of software that automatically replies to e-mail. This is commonly used by employees in large companies if they are going to be out of the office for an extended amount of time).

MTA. Mail Transfer Agent (Server).

MUA. Mail User Agent (client).

Pessimal. Maximally bad; the obvious Latin-based antonym for "optimal," but for some reason it does not appear in most English dictionaries.

Ping. Test to see if the other person is there /awake/available. This comes from a Unix test to see if a machine (or its net connection) was active or not. "Coffee tomorrow? I may be busy with a client. Ping me at noon or so."

Post. Send to a distribution list or Usenet news group, i.e. to a quasi-stable group of people.

Intel's 10 Commandments of E-Mail

1. Don't use your inbox as a catchall folder for everything you need to work on.
2. Create a "Five Weeks" folder that deletes its contents automatically after five weeks.
3. Assist colleagues' inbox-filtering efforts by agreeing on acronyms to use in subject lines that identify important messages.
4. Send group mail only when it is useful to all recipients.
5. Ask to be removed from distribution lists that you don't need to be on.
6. Traveling? Use your e-mail's "out-of-office" feature.
7. When possible, send a message that is only a subject line, so recipients don't have to open the e-mail to read a single line. End the subject line with <EOM>, the acronym for End of Message.
8. Use graphics and attachments sparingly.
9. Put attachments larger than 5MB on the company's Web site or intranet.
10. Be specific. If you send a 20-page attachment, tell the recipient that the important information is on pages 2 and 17.

– *American Way, June 15, 2001*

Chapter 5

International E-Mail

Around the World in 80 Seconds

Several years ago my husband was working in Kazakhstan. While staying at an old Soviet health sanitarium outside of the capital city of Almaty that had been converted to a hotel, he was told of another American businessman's adventures there. One day this businessman was stuck in an elevator during one of the frequent power outages. Although it was dark and he was alone in the stalled elevator, at first he was unconcerned since he knew from experience that the power failures were usually brief. However, as time passed he became more concerned and started banging on the door and calling for help. Eventually he remembered seeing a telephone on the control panel and felt around in the dark until he located it. It was an older rotary dial handset so it was fairly easy to dial "O" for "Operator" in the dark. Soon he was connected to the Front Desk of the hotel and the desk clerk answered, "Da, ya slushayu (Yes, I'm listening)." The American was relieved and began to rapidly tell the desk clerk that he was trapped in the elevator. And the Russian clerk answered, "Da, ya slushayu." This exchange was repeated several times until it became clear that the Russian and the American did not speak the other's language. At this point the line went dead as the clerk ran off to find someone who could speak English. In due time, another voice came on the line asking in accented English, "Da, can I help you?" The American explained he was trapped in the elevator and the Russian replied that they were working on the problem and expected to have the elevator running again in 30 minutes. The American then said, "What am I supposed to do for the next 30 minutes?' The Russian answered, "You might try studying some Russian" and hung up. The moral of this story is, when in Rome, it helps to speak Italian.

With the universal use of e-mail, we can now communicate without the expense of international phone calls and overnight mail delivery, which often is lost or never arrives.

We need to realize that although e-mail is a very cost effective way to conduct business all over the world and beats other various forms of communication, special consideration and respect need to be paid to our international e-mails. We need to be aware of the difference in time zones, customs, and local cultural holidays. We should be aware that although technology in the United States has advanced rapidly, in many other parts of the world it has not. Just because we expect a fast reply, doesn't make it so. Let's consider the following:

:-) VERY IMPORTANT: Be very careful about using humor, sarcasm and slang terms over e-mail.

The translation may not be understood and a misinterpretation can be harmful to a relationship. Common slang expressions that are used everyday by Americans can be baffling to others and mean something entirely different in another language. I remember when my Asian nail technician was giving me a pedicure and I laughed at something she said. I replied to her, "Oh, you're pulling my leg!" She stopped immediately and apologized, saying, "I am sorry. I didn't mean to hurt your leg!" We are already dealing with the lack of facial expression and body language and now factor in the differences in cultures. Some things do not translate well.

:-) Although most homes and offices in the United States have computers with e-mail capabilities, many other countries do not enjoy such a luxury. Allow ample time for your e-mail message to be received and reviewed and practice patience when expecting a reply to your "urgent" message.

:-) Make allowances for the difference in time zones between countries.

:-) Be sure to include the date and time you send your e-mail. It is best to use military time when sending international correspondence as this is more commonly recognized in other parts of the world. The date should be sent as DAY—

MONTH—YEAR. i.e., July 25, 2002 would be: 25-07-2002

:-) Include complete contact information including your international country code, area code, address, country, and zip code with your signature. Some business will still need to be conducted over the telephone, fax or through the mail. Make it easy for the receiver to contact you.

:-) Many circumstances, including weather, may render phone lines inoperable. Be patient in waiting for a reply.

:-) Not all countries use the American dollar in negotiating contracts or other agreements, so be aware of the local currency regulations or customs. Take the time to determine if there are any regulations mandating or requiring the use of local currency or if there are strong prevailing local customs favoring hard currencies.

:-) Use the correct characters for correct spelling of peoples' names and places. i.e., José, André, Malmö, Valdepeñas

:-) Thinking in advance about the contents and purpose of your e-mail correspondence can save face . . . your face.

:-) Be aware of holidays in other countries. We tend to forget that holidays in foreign countries do not correspond to those in the United States.

THINK first.
WRITE second.
SPELL CHECK third.
PROOFREAD fourth.
LISTEN to your own e-mail message by reading it out loud to see how it will come across to the receiver. And lastly,
RE-EVALUATE before pressing "send now."

The Internet is a place to learn and have fun. We make it more enjoyable for ourselves and our fellow "Netizens" by being courteous and polite. The Internet is a vast community of people from all over the world. In this global electronic community, people's impression of you is based on the quality of your writing. A thorough knowledge of Netiquette will prevent misunderstandings.

Chapter 6

Instant Messaging

Jargon, Jabber and Rap, Oh My!

Only in America do people order double cheeseburgers, large fries and a diet soda.

Only in America do we leave cars worth thousands of dollars in the driveway and leave useless things and other junk boxes in the garage.

Only in America do banks leave both doors open and then chain the pens to the counter.

Only in America can a pizza get to your house faster than an ambulance.

. . . And only in America do we crave Instant Communication and pray for a special letter to be delivered by "snail mail!"

Instant Messaging is an on-line one-on-one chat. I personally have a love/hate relationship with this feature. Thinking positive, it's nice to be able to carry on a conversation immediately with my children who live in other states, talk for hours, and not pay long distance telephone rates. Instant Messaging is a new culture that gives computer users instant gratification with real-time communication. Instant Messaging or "IM" as it is commonly referred to, is extremely popular with pre-teens and teenagers and is one of today's main modes of communication for them. In my teen years, we rushed home from school and immediately picked up the telephone. As I remember it, I was often yelled at for talking on the phone too much and too long. When it was time for Dad to issue a punishment, (as if I ever did anything to deserve it!) The first thing he took away was my telephone privileges.

Additionally, Instant Messaging has become increasingly popular in the business community. I believe that one of the greatest advantages in using Instant Messaging in business is that you avoid the delays with usual e-mail messages, phone calls, faxes and certainly "snail mail." It can be a very useful tool and a great concept. Instead of "talking one-on-one" you are "writing one-on-one." Also, Instant Messaging ensures that your message was received, which is vital in our fast-paced business environment today.

Don't Interrupt

One of the biggest negatives that I have heard most often is how easily Instant Messaging can be intrusive upon one's work time. Senders with even the best of intentions will interrupt projects and important work with unnecessary messages or they just want to talk. Some programs allow you to block Instant Messaging or you can ignore the Instant Messaging call. The problem with not responding, of course, is that the sender can see that you are online and ignoring their "call." This can be considered to be rude behavior. To prevent ill feelings, my suggestion is to respond, "Good to hear from you. I am working on a project that needs my undivided concentration. Let me call you later!" And then, DO call later. Do what you say you are going to do.

Don't Be Annoying

Instant Messaging can be annoying without observing a few courtesies. Be aware that not all people have the time to carry on a conversation while they are at work or concentrating on something.

Be Thoughtful

Be understanding if you Instant Message someone and they do not respond or they tell you they are working on a project and will call you later.

Teens have their own "jargon" that they use when they communicate on Instant Messaging, but as adults and especially if we are conducting business, we need to be aware of sticking with the rules of writing.

The same rules for writing apply with Instant Messaging as well as e-mail:

:-) Capitalize the beginning of your sentences.

:-) Watch your spelling, punctuation and grammar.

:-) Wait for a response.

:-) Don't send long involved messages.

:-) Remember that Instant Messaging is for brief chats, not lengthy letters.

:-) Call and talk if you have something confidential or important to discuss.

:-) Do not hit "send" after every few words. Wait until you complete the thought.

Companies that provide Instant Messaging capabilities claim that messages can't be intercepted by a third person. I am not so sure I believe this as I have been told that some major corporations actually hire people to trace and record e-mails, faxes, etc. and will retrieve messages being sent and received at work. With that in mind, be cautious of what you say, how you say it, who you talk about and your language. My rule of thumb goes back to something that my grandmother always told me. She used to say, "Never put anything in writing that you don't want to see on the front page of the newspaper."

Chapter 7

Emoticons

Smileys, Grins, Smirks and Sneers

A doctor who had devoted his life to helping the underprivileged lived over a liquor store in the poor section of a large city. In front of the liquor store was a simple sign reading "Dr. Williams is upstairs."

When he died, the doctor had no relatives and he left no money for his burial. He had never asked for payment from anyone he had ever treated. Friends and patients scraped together enough money to bury the good doctor, but they had no money for a tombstone. It appeared his grave was going to be unmarked until someone came up with a wonderful suggestion.

They took the sign from in front of the liquor store and nailed it to a post over his grave. It made a lovely epitaph: Dr. Williams is upstairs.

Signs and symbols have always been part of our lives and are used universally. Emoticons are cyberspace signs, symbols and acronyms. They are the "shorthand" of cyberspace. Emoticon is "cybergeekspeak" for an icon that expresses emotion. They are supposed to convey an emotion to the recipient.

Emoticons have been created to add voice inflections, facial expressions and body language to your e-mail messages. Although they are fun to use, their main purpose is avoiding misinterpretation of the writer's intentions.

We must remember that Emoticons are really meant for casual e-mail rather than business correspondence. In business, your recipient may construe using Emoticons as childish and unprofessional.

Emoticons have become so popular that several Websites have been developed just for collecting them. There are Emoticons for celebrities, basic Smiley faces, special emotion Smileys, animals, professions, phrases and entire sentences.

Emoticons can convey many emotions through very creative symbols, all of which are simple keystrokes on our keyboards. They can send messages including, smiles, laughs, happiness, teasing, being a bit mischievous, affirming, anger, being sarcastic and feelings of surprise.

Teens have developed some of their own "shorthand" and Emoticons that they use in e-mail as well as their Instant Messaging, which you can refer to in the Appendix.

Have you ever received e-mail messages and wondered what the writer really meant? Was he or she being sarcastic, funny or serious? This is where Emoticons come into play. They are truly the body language and voice inflection needed in e-mail.

The real trick of understanding Emoticons is to turn your head about 90° to the left. A Smiley face (the most common Emoticon used) is a colon, followed by a closing parenthesis. :) You can even add a nose :-) or make Smiley wink . ;-) Of course, the sad Smiley is :(and you can give a sad Smiley a nose. :-(I personally like the person laughing out loud. :-D The acronym for laughing out loud is "LOL." The acronyms I see used most often is "BRB" (Be Right Back) and "BTW" (By The Way).

We don't all have the same handwriting or the same emotional expressions and we do not have to have the same e-mail style. Emoticons are a great way to add personal touches to your online correspondence. Additionally, you can use different fonts, colors, links, photos, and other graphical images.

Please refer to the Appendices for some great ideas on Emoticons and e-mail shorthand. Add pizzazz to your casual correspondence!

Chapter 8

Fax Finesse

Nothing But the Fax, Ma'am!

A minister was opening his mail one morning. Drawing a single sheet of paper from an envelope with no return address, he found written on it only one word: "FOOL."

The next Sunday, he announced during his services, "I have known many people who have written letters and forgotten to sign their names. However, this week I received a letter from someone who signed his name and had forgotten to write a letter."

Great perspective of interpretation, wouldn't you say? It happens so often in the world. Someone has something to say, but tries to hide his identity. This is the way that I view FAX ADVERTISING. I personally do not like or appreciate unsolicited advertising of any kind, including fax advertising. It's such a waste of good paper and expensive toner! Every day when I come into the office, my fax machine has filled during the night with a barrage of advertising. I can't even imagine the money that companies have spent to do this type of advertising. It is worthless. I never read the advertising. I have a box that I put it into and use the other side for scrap paper. I hate waste, so this is the only way that I have found that I can recycle the unsolicited paper. This practice is actually illegal in some states.

The FCC (Federal Communication Commission) states the rule as follows: "Unsolicited advertisements may not be transmitted by any device to a telephone facsimile machine unless the person receiving the facsimile has given prior express invitation or permission to receive it. If the sender and the recipient have an established business relationship, an invitation or permission to receive unsolicited facsimile advertisements is presumed to exist. However, the recipient may end an established business relationship by requesting that no further unsolicited advertisements be sent, thus revoking any invitation or permission to receive further transmissions."

In December of 2001, The Dallas Cowboys settled a class action lawsuit over junk faxes for $1.73 million. A Dallas-based company, American Blastfax, Inc., sent faxes to 125,000 individuals and companies on two separate occasions in December of 1999 to advertise the team's playoff tickets. Omnibus International received the unwanted fax and sued the Dallas Cowboys, alleging that the unsolicited junk faxes hurt legitimate advertising as well as consumers and businesses. The Omnibus complaint was combined with others to form the class action. Under the settlement, the recipients are eligible for up to $500 for each unsolicited transmission. Wow! I wish I had kept my copy!

What is the lesson or the bottom line here? Simple: Never send unsolicited faxes.

I lived in Indonesia from 1989 to 1991 and prior to going, I worked for a law firm in California. We never used a fax machine. I'm not sure if they were even invented then!

When I returned from Indonesia, EVERY law firm was using one. When I went to work for a law firm in Texas, the fax machine boggled my mind. It seemed so "technologically advanced." Facsimile machines had become as common in the work place as the office copier. I found that a facsimile machine was a great way to expedite the transmission of documents and information.

"Thanks to the fax machine, one can expedite documents across the nation in a very cost efficient manner resulting in the prompt execution of legal documents without requiring everyone to be at the same place at the same time."

—HARMON J. NORTON,
INVESTMENT REPRESENTATIVE FOR EDWARD JONES

In a few short years the facsimile machine had made a definite impact in the communication industry. Even with the arrival of the Internet, we still use fax machines daily and I don't believe that they will become obsolete any time soon. Facsimile machines serve a great purpose.

Traditionally, fax machines are freestanding with a dedicated phone line. Some businesses and homes now use a computer fax, which is based on a specifically programmed modem installed within the computer.

There are basic principles of courtesy so that the system works smoothly. Here are a few of those guiding principles.

- First, learn the proper way to use them. If you guess wrong, you could inconvenience many others.
- Your word is your bond. If you say you are going to send something via fax, send it and send it *when* you say you are going to send it.
- Remember that although this is a speedy way to communicate, don't get careless with your faxes. They should reflect your professionalism just as your written correspondence should.
- Call in advance to see if you need to include a COVER PAGE. I would suggest that you do this as a matter of habit anyway. I also like to make my cover page with a little larger font size and I emphasize the intended receiver's name by typing it in bold or all caps. This helps when one fax machine is being shared by several recipients.
- Always include your contact information on your cover page to provide the recipient a quick reference tool for a quick reply. I get faxes that do not include a phone number or return fax number. For the convenience of the receiving party, always include this kind of information and make it easy to find. The infor-

mation that should be on your cover sheet should include a line describing the subject of the fax, the receiver's name, sender's name, date, number of pages being transmitted, and a brief description of what is included in the fax.

- As stated above, I like to use a larger font for my cover page, but I always include a confidentiality statement at the bottom of my cover sheet that is in a much smaller font. Although I am NOT giving you legal advice, following is the confidentiality notice I use.

Confidentiality Notice

The documents accompanying this facsimile communication contain confidential information that is legally privileged. The information is intended for the use of the intended recipient named above. If you are not the intended recipient, you are hereby notified that any disclosure, copying, distribution or taking of any action in reliance on the contents of this telecopied information except its direct delivery to the intended recipient named above is strictly prohibited. If you have received this fax in error, please notify us immediately by telephone to arrange for the return of the original document to us.

- Colored paper does not fax very well. If you use correction fluid, it will show up as a blotch.
- Keep a receipt of the transmission. You may need to refer to it in the future. I learned this the hard way. I ordered my season tickets for the Dallas Summer Musicals and they said they never received the transmission. I had no proof as I had always thrown away the receipts of each fax transmission. So after being season ticket holders for several years, I lost my great seats because I couldn't show proof that I had ordered them over the fax machine.
- CALL AHEAD! Notify the intended recipient that the fax is being sent. Often in large corporations fax machines are shared and to assure that the correct party receives your transmission, let them know in advance that it is on its way. This also gives you the opportunity to verify the fax number before you hit "send."
- CALL TO CONFIRM! If you are sending important information over the fax machine, you want to verify the intended party received the information. I know you are saying, "But this is supposed to *save* me making those calls!" No, the purpose of the fax is to send information swiftly. Therefore, we need to make sure the correct party receives it.
- Be considerate about sending lengthy documents. The rule of thumb is to never send more

than five pages at a time. More pages transmitted at once can tie up a fax machine for a long time and use a lot of paper. Make sure the recipient knows how many pages you are sending and will want them all. This also gives them a chance to check their machine to make sure there is enough paper and toner to receive your transmission. Recently, I returned to my office after being on the road for a week when a sender had transmitted an unsolicited 50-page document that used all of my paper. As a result, I did not receive any other transmissions while my office was closed.

- Be aware that a lot of facsimile machines may cut off pertinent information if the margins are not about 1½" on the top, bottom, and sides of the paper you are transmitting.
- Finally, before you hit the "send" button, stop and check that you have the correct name and phone number for the recipient. This is especially true if you use speed dial buttons. The danger here is obvious—make a mistake and hit the wrong button and the fax will go to the wrong recipient. If the fax contains confidential material, you may be in big trouble.

Although this may seem too obvious, it does happen. In fact, my husband's company did this a few years ago and it cost them several thousand dollars to retrieve an errant fax. My husband was part of a team negotiating a contract with the government of Turkmenistan. They were in Ashgabat, Turkmenistan preparing to open negotiations. After the final draft of the proposal was prepared, a secretary in London was called and asked to fax a copy to another office for a final review. She called back a few minutes later in a state of panic. Instead of sending the contract to the intended office, she had mistakenly hit the adjacent speed dial button and the contract was now in the office of one of their competitors, in Istanbul, Turkey no less.

Fortunately, it was late Sunday evening, so there was no one at the other office to read the proposal. This problem was resolved by putting one of the team members on the next plane from Ashgabat to Istanbul so that he could be on the doorstep when the office was opened Monday morning. After explaining what had happened, he was allowed to retrieve the proposal from the fax machine before anyone in the office had a chance to read it. One result of this episode was that all phone numbers were removed from the speed dial of the faxes on the London office.

Bottom line: Think before you fax!

Chapter 9

Cell Phone Courtesies

No More Cell Yell!

The moon was slowly setting in the western sky while the sun was rising in the east. I was sitting at my favorite morning breakfast place along with other customers who clamored to get those hot-out-of-the-oven breakfast delights. I was looking out of the window as vanilla glaze and cinnamon were swirling in my mouth from the best cinnamon roll I had ever tasted when I noticed a young executive pull up in a brand-new Jaguar XKE.

Reeking of success, our young executive straightened out his obviously very expensive Armani suit. At the same time, he was carrying on quite an animated conversation on his cell phone. He stepped in, sat down, and grabbed a menu, while never losing a beat in the mobile conversation. He pointed to something on the menu and indicated to the frustrated waitress to "hurry it up!" Then, Mr. Important, in a loud, cell-yell voice, insisted that his order be shipped overnight and, "Of course, I will pay for the extra service!" He then gave his credit card number, expiration date, and address and spelled his name. Hmmmmmmmmmm . . .

Sitting very close to Mr. VIP was another customer. He didn't look quite as well dressed. Fact is, I wondered when I looked at him how he could afford the coffee he was drinking. But something else interesting caught my eye. He was feverishly writing something down on a napkin. Hmmmmmmmmmmm . . . .

A few days later, I was sitting in my usual corner of the bakery, when Mr. VIP drove up again, ordered a dozen bagels to-go and handed the clerk his credit card. Within seconds, she handed the card back and said it had been declined. "Declined!!!!" Mr. Important yelled. "That can't be! That card has more than $10,000 worth of credit on it!" The clerk ran the card again. The card was once again declined. He paid cash and stormed out.

Just then, I noticed the same gentleman who could barely afford the coffee a few days ago in a new set of clothes, with a cell phone, laptop computer, full breakfast and grinning from ear-to-ear. Hmmmmmmmmmm . . .

Okay, maybe it didn't happen just like that, but it is a fact that people are yelling in public places on their cell phones and giving out their credit card numbers along with all other pertinent information which makes it extremely easy for anyone to steal. I know you are thinking that it is stupid for anyone with a brain to be yelling his or her credit card numbers and personal information in public, but it happens every day.

It seems that it was only yesterday people used to go on vacations to get away from the phone. Now, everyone takes his or her phone with them! I think there was only a five-minute lag time between the purchase of the first cell phone and the establishment of etiquette rules against using this great invention in a restaurant, during a concert, in the library, or during a religious service.

> **"Folks sometimes forget to turn off their cell phone when they're in church, meetings, or restaurants. Then, when it rings, they sit there, embarrassed and pretending it is somebody else's while it rings and rings. They need to learn how to press just one simple button to stop the ringing until it rolls over to voice mail!"**
>
> —HAL DAVIS, ATTORNEY

This doesn't seem to negate the fact that rude people, in fact, do keep their cell phones on in these establishments along with many other "unacceptable" places.

> **"I've heard cell phones ringing during formal church services. What's up with that!?"**
>
> —JIM SUNDELIUS, UNITED SECURITIES ALLIANCE, INC.

We have all heard the excuses for the rude use of cell phones that range anywhere from urgent personal reasons to a business crises. I believe these excuses are overused and misused and just not acceptable any longer. If you feel the need to keep your cell phone on for work or personal reasons in places where it may intrude on others, then you need to turn them off, turn them on vibrate, or stay home or in your office to receive these urgent calls.

> **"I hate cell phones ringing on the golf course. It's so rude!"**
>
> —YOLANDA GOTTHARDT, AFLAC, INC.

When cell phones first became popular, people of "self-proclaimed importance" were the only ones who carried them. I remember when I moved to Texas in 1991 and bought a new car that one of the "perks" was receiving a discounted mobile phone and one free month's service. My husband and I went to the office to pick up the phone and discovered the monthly fee and the "per-minute" usage was exorbitant. We turned the "deal" down.

Just a few months after this time, I decided to open my own business and found myself on the road a lot and not being the type of person who likes (or feels safe) stopping at gas stations to make calls, I decided to invest in a mobile phone. It has proven to be a great investment.

According to the U.S. Census Bureau, four in ten Americans used a cellular telephone in the year 2000. These statistics show that there were about five million subscribers in 1990, compared to 110 million subscribers just ten years later. Why? Because over the decade, the cell phone has become more affordable, with the average monthly bill decreasing from $81 to $45. David Pearce Snyder, lifestyles editor of *The Futurist*, said that in 10 to 15 years, 80 percent of the population will carry a cell phone and it will be the only phone they use.

As the statistics show, more and more people own mobile phones. You see kids from elementary age to grandparents with mobile phones stuck in their ears in the malls, the movies, libraries, walking down the street and in the car. I was recently teaching my "High-Tech Etiquette" seminar to 30 sophomores in high school and I asked, "How many of you have a personal cell phone?" Twenty-eight hands shot up! I was floored. When I was a teenager, I was lucky to have phone "privileges!"

Mobile phones have become such a phenomenon that the number of cell phone users will more than double by 2003, from 69 million to 150 million, according to the Cellular Telecommunications Industry Association, and advertising is expected to be a $1.2 billion market. Additionally, a recent survey conducted by a major wireless company states that more than 54% of American families now have one or more wireless phones and predict that by the end of the year 2002 more than 90% of American families will own one or more wireless phones (*USA Today*, February 16, 2000).

Think about it—we are a mobile society. A cell phone can connect us to the Internet and can accomplish many purposes for everyone in all walks of life. While a mom is at her daughter's ice skating competition, she can transfer cash into her checking account and pay her utility bill. A specialty basket and gift shop owner sends a message to her customers, letting them know that she is offering a 25% discount on all holiday baskets. A salesman checks his cell phone display and sees that his company's iron widgets are overstocked, so now he can offer his customer a great deal.

Cell phones are a great new electronic device. However, I feel that along with being the owner of a mobile phone, comes the responsibility of using it with courtesy. I just left a dinner where a guest's cell phone went off during the meeting, while the speaker was addressing the audience . . . not once, but twice! Okay, so you accidentally leave your cell phone on when the meeting starts, but PLEASE turn it off after you realize your mistake!!

Worse than the two calls, however, was the fact that this gentleman (I am using that term loosely) carried on a full conversation with the callers. Since I was unfortunately sitting at the same table with him, may I assure you that neither conversation was an emergency. He wasn't wearing a fireman's hat, a police cap, or sporting a stethoscope, so I assume he wasn't on emergency duty!

Then there was the day the mobile phone when off in the library, the theater, the movies, the graduation ceremony, the bookstore, the grocery store, the airplane, church, the concert hall, the football stadium, school, funeral . . . . Talking about funerals . . . Did you hear about the funeral in Sweden where during the service, a cell phone kept going off? Annoyed, the minister asked whose cell phone was ringing. When no one confessed and the phone kept ringing, the mourners started a search to find where the ringing was coming from. Much to their surprise, they found it coming from inside the coffin. It appeared the deceased had been buried with his cell phone in his suit pocket, still turned on. Gives a whole new meaning to, "The cellular customer you are trying to reach is unavailable at this time." It appears the battery lasted longer than the deceased!

One of the worst times that I remember a mobile phone ringing was at a major luncheon sponsored by the Plano Chamber of Commerce in Plano, Texas. It was an extra special luncheon as it was not only celebrating the successes of the outstanding Ambassadors of the Chamber, but it was also the Leadership Plano Graduation Ceremony. The Mayor was giving the graduation address when a cell phone rang . . . at my table. The man (not a friend, just a guy) answered the phone and proceeded to carry on a full conversation that went something like this: "Oh, hi, honey! Just having lunch with a few friends. Uh, huh. Uh, huh. Did you get that new Beanie Baby at McDonald's today? No? Well, I'll stop by when I leave here and pick it up. The food here was pretty bad, so I'm still hungry. Uh, huh. Uh, huh. No, it's no problem. I'll pick up some chicken for dinner. Uh, huh. Well, tell her I'll help her with her spelling test when I get home. Uh, huh. I love you too. Bye, bye now."

CAN YOU BELIEVE THIS!!?? Never have I seen a more rude person. Did he think he appeared important? Did he think what he was doing was acceptable or polite? Did he think he wasn't disturbing anyone around him, let alone the Mayor? What could have possibly been going through his mind? We'll never know what he thought, but the people around him thought HE was an IDIOT!

> **"It is not only annoying, it is rude to be subjected to someone's personal business while standing in line or shopping in a store. I once had to hear a young woman discuss her father's divorce and her own emotional problems while I tried to locate a book on the shelf . . . unreal!!"**
>
> **—MARY MILLHOLLAND, AUTHOR AND GRAPHIC DESIGNER**

My son, Terry, works in retail and he complains that it irritates him that people are talking on their mobile phones when he is actively trying to assist them. Not only is the sales clerk irritated, but so are the waiting customers who feel this unthoughtful person isn't concentrating on the transaction and is taking too long to process their credit card, write a check, or count cash.

It is reasonable and courteous to expect a customer to pay full attention to the service provider and it is discourteous of a customer to hold up other customers with their personal phone calls, which can only distract their actions. Additionally, Terry tells me that people are always complaining about "poor customer service." In defense of the customer service provider and in Terry's words, "How can I ask, 'Is there anything else I can help you with?' when it is considered rude to interrupt someone that is on the phone?" It is a dilemma that most customer service people face. Basically, if you are the customer, get off the phone when at a check stand and pay attention to what is going on around you. This will save a lot of people behind you and the clerk a lot of irritation.

Now, with all that being said, I have to tell you one of the funniest experiences regarding a cell phone user that I have personally witnessed. My daughters, Julie and Lorie, my Aunt Norma, and I were at a coffee shop in Memphis, Tennessee on a "girls vacation" to Graceland. The customer service experience that we encountered on that warm summer night is one that belongs in the archives of "Ripley's Believe it or Not" museum. Just to mention ONE of the acts that occurred was that of a cell phone user. No, it was not the customer . . . it was the waitress! As she was pouring coffee, taking orders, delivering food, she never once quit talking on her cell phone. She was shouting, laughing, cussing, and was basically unaware of how irritated her customers and everyone else was in the restaurant. Every now and then she would scream, "Just a minute, Lucy!" and then yell across the restaurant, " Hey, mister, you want some cream with that coffee?" This IS a true story!

LESSONS OF GENERAL CELL PHONE USE

Lesson One

TURN OFF YOUR CELL PHONE when you are in a public forum and people are gathered to listen to a speaker, an entertainer, enjoy each other's company or paid entertainment. Turn your cell phones off when you are attending a meeting. Even a muttered conversation in the middle of a meeting is just plain bad manners. Most cellular phones have a silence mode and if they don't, turn them completely off. If you are expecting an emergency phone call, put your phone on the vibrate or silence mode or carry a beeper that has those features. If you are expecting a call from your office or family, let them know that you will be unavailable from 12:00 to 1:00 or however long the meeting will last. Another possibility is to let them know the phone number of the meeting place. Have them call there and ask an attendant to find you. Alert the attendant to the possibility of an emergency call and sit where the attendant can easily find you without disturbing the meeting. This takes planning in advance, but it is the courteous thing to do. Make it a practice.

Remember the days when parents went to a public phone during breaks, intermission or after the entree and before the dessert and called home to check with the babysitter? No? Well, it used to work fine. Step into the lobby and make your call.

Lesson Two

Understand the features on your phone. Read the manual! Get to know how to use redial, speed dial, and other features.

Lesson Three

Tick-Tock . . . the clock is running! Do not call someone on their cellular phone without their permission. Although rates are getting better, each call is still expensive and the minutes add up fast. Plan your calls during office hours. I have one friend who loves to call me on my cell phone and talk for hours even when I am home or in my office. I simply tell him to let me call him back from my land phone. Discuss only pressing issues. Save the rest for office calls.

Lesson Four

Avoid putting cell phone users on hold. When I have been put on hold, I just see the clock spinning and money flying.

Lesson Five

Just as you should when placing any call, identify yourself with your first (and sometimes last) name. Always ask if it is a good time to talk. Additionally, when receiving a call, identify yourself.

Lesson Six

It is just as rude to be eating, chewing, or chomping while you are talking on a cell phone as it is when you are talking on a regular land line telephone. Even though it is convenient to go through the drive-through, order your lunch, pay the attendant, get the sack, and drive on, it doesn't mean your listener wants to hear all of this external conversation and then hear you chewing your Big Mac!

The Rules of Safe Cellular Phone Use in the Car

Now let's address the cell phone use in cars. Many of us have suffered the loss of a loved one because of a traffic fatality. Just recently a very dear friend, only 52 years old, was killed when he turned into traffic while talking on his cell phone. He was killed instantly and the accident was his fault. Undoubtedly, he was distracted while talking to a client explaining he was going to be late for their meeting. How very sad for his family and friends that he never made that meeting and will never see his wife, children, or grandchildren again.

In 1997, there were 57 traffic fatalities in which police noted that cellular phones had played a part in the accident. That number has been multiplied by an alarming percentage each year thereafter. The National Safety Council states that drivers with a phone in their car run a 34% higher risk of having a collision.

The National Highway Traffic Safety Association suggests pulling off of the road before using a cell phone or reading a beeper. "At 55 miles an hour, things can go wrong very quickly," says Tim Hurd, NHTSA Chief of media relations. "It's best to have your full attention on driving." If you must use the phone while driving, heed the following rules.

Rule One

Pull off of the road when talking on your cell phone so you can focus on the road and traffic when you are driving. Do not engage in stressful or emotional conversations that may divert your attention from the road.

Rule Two

Preprogram your phone with numbers that you call frequently. Another option that is quickly becoming popular is the use of a hands-free device. I believe that laws are just minutes away from being passed that will require hands-free devices for cellular phones in cars. With the fatality rates soaring and the use of cellular phones being the cause, it is inevitable that legislation will be necessary to control this driving hazard.

Rule Three

Avoid distractions. Let the person to whom you are speaking know that you are driving. In case you get cut off or fade in and out, the listener knows why. If you lose your connection, it is the responsibility of the person who originated the call to call back.

Rule Four

Always—always—end the call when you find yourself in heavy traffic, construction areas, and hazardous weather conditions. Keep your hands, eyes, and mind on the road.

Rule Five

Never try to take notes while you are driving. Pull over or use a dictation device that is easy to use.

Rule Six

Turn off your car radio and roll up your windows to help eliminate background noise. Keep the air conditioner on low.

Rule Seven

Speak clearly and directly into the mouthpiece or headset in the car. No matter how much you try to reduce the outside noises, some will come through. However, do not blast out your listener's ears by being too loud. Remember that even the best cell phone is subject to not always having a good connection. If the connection is not good, don't try to yell your way through your conversation. Also, if you know of certain areas where you do not get good reception, be kind to the caller and let their message go into voice mail so you can return their call when they can better hear you.

Rule Eight

When you have passengers in the car, avoid using your phone. If you are the passenger, also refrain from using your cell phone in the car. This can be extremely distracting to the driver.

Even with all the rules of courtesy that should be observed, please understand that cellular phones are a wonderful invention and I am very happy I have one. It is a great safety device for when your car breaks down, you have a flat tire, or for other emergencies that you might encounter. Over 140,000 calls are placed to emergency services every day from cell phones. They serve an important purpose. I have personally purchased cell phones for both of my daughters and my parents for just that reason. However, being courteous while driving is extremely important.

"Road Rage" has been attributed to many causes and cell phone users have been one of the reasons people become angry. It is a fact that no matter how good a driver you may be (or think you are) when distracted by talking on the phone, you slow down, speed up, drive out of your lane, miss traffic lights changing, etc. People get furious over these infractions.

Thumping watermelons in the grocery while talking on the cell phone or walking down the street engaging in an animated conversation looks ridiculous. If you must, pretend you are Superman and escape into a phone booth or private area to complete your conversation if it is really essential and can't wait until you are at home or in the office.

Many restaurants have started adding to their non-smoking and smoking sections a "cellular phone usage section." Funny, but true! Wouldn't it have been nice for Mr. Important to have a private area to make his call? Maybe his credit card information wouldn't have been stolen . . . and then again, maybe it still would have! Guess we will never know.

Let me offer one last thought on cell phones that is important for you to keep in mind. Cellular phones are not private and people do have listening devices that can tune into your conversation. These strangers have been known to record calls and use the information for perverted reasons. Be careful what you say. It can come back to haunt you.

The bottom line: cell phones are just electronic equipment. It's the cell phone users that are rude, not the cell phone. It's up to the owners to use the etiquette rules against making disturbing noise, by shouting, speaking when it is an interruption to another activity, conducting business at social occasions, or ignoring the actual presence of people to whom one is expected to give one's attention.

The Top Ten Rude Rings

1. Eating, chewing or drinking while on the phone.
2. Taking a call during a meeting or in a public forum.
3. Not excusing yourself to take a personal, sensitive or extended call.
4. Ignoring the ringing! If you hear it, answer it or turn it off!
5. Taking numerous calls while meeting with someone. When you are with someone, they are the priority.
6. Putting cell phone callers on hold without waiting for permission.
7. Placing and taking calls in a noisy location.
8. Phones that play theme songs or novelty songs for their ring.
9. Taking calls while driving and not being able to write important information or concentrate. Better to call later when you can write important data down.
10. Keeping others waiting while you finish your conversation.

Chapter 10

Telephone Protocol

Swimming Through the Abyss

If you want . . . please press 1. If you want . . . please press 2. If you want . . . please press 5. If you want . . . please press 7. If you want . . . please press 4. If you want . . . please press 11. If you want . . . please press 3. If you want . . . please press 6. If you want . . . please press 12. If you want . . . please press 1. If you want . . . please press . . . I'm sorry, the extension you are trying to reach is not valid. Please call back. CLINK!!

Sound familiar? It's a sign of the times . . . it's called "automation." I call it "the Abyss." An abyss is a chasm, vacuum, void, space, cavity, gulf, hole, pit, crevasse or a bottomless pit! Isn't that what some companies have installed and have the nerve to call it "customer care!!" I stand on the ground that if companies cared, they would staff their offices so that I could speak to a human. Of course, I would also train the people answering the phones to have pleasant voices, good attitudes and good customer service skills. I am really asking a lot, aren't I?

The truth is, The Abyss is a fact of life. It has become more and more difficult, if not close to impossible, to reach a human today and I think it's going to get worse before it gets better.

I called a company last week and asked for Ms. Smith. (The name has been changed to protect the innocent.) The receptionist apologized for Ms. Smith's absence, but said she would be happy to take a message. I was stunned! I asked, "You mean YOU are going to write down my message? Don't you mean that you will transfer me to her voice mail so I can LEAVE a message?" She laughed and said that her company didn't believe in the voice mail system and she takes all of the messages the old fashioned way. I was so excited! Then I thought . . . I hope she gets it right! After all, if I leave a message and it's wrong, it's my fault. Now I have to allow for human error. I immediately made a mental note to self: "Make sure you call back tomorrow to confirm she received my *correct* message."

> **"My greatest joy is when I place a telephone call and a live person answers the call and directs me to the party I wish to speak to."**
>
> —PETER KRAUSE, THE INSURANCE HOUSE

First, we must realize that building rapport over the phone isn't the easiest thing one has to do. We loose approximately 30% of our energy when we are speaking over the phone, not to mention the loss of facial expressions and body language. It is, therefore, imperative that our first impression is a good lasting impression.

I have heard many complaints from callers that phone systems go on and on with little or no option for your specific question or inquiry. If you must use a phone tree, build it with the caller mind. Allow early options and don't force all callers to listen to the entire menu before they can proceed.

> **"I hate phone systems that don't allow you an easy way out and the ones that give you tons of information before giving you an option to actually contact someone!"**
>
> **—TERRY SEEFLUTH, PARTYLITE CANDLES AND GIFTS**

Although a ton of business is being conducted over the Internet today, we still rely on using office phones and then mix in cell phones, conference calls, and speakerphones.

A key to successful phone use is to simply remember that your caller cannot see you. Your challenge is to make up for all that lost nonverbal communication by using your voice effectively.

The tone and attitude of our voice is immediately heard and mentally processed by the listener when we answer or place a call. Do you want to really know what you sound like? Record your voice and play it back. I suggest you record it at various times during the day for a true test. I have yet to meet a person that doesn't say, "I don't sound like that!" Well, yes you do! And one of the critical elements of telephone communication is your voice variety and tone. I would never minimize the importance of the words you use, but I assure you that your tone will determine what the listener really hears or perceives they hear.

We speak at approximately 120–150 words per minute and listen at 400–600 words per minute. People in various regions across the United States speak at different rates. Southerners are known to speak a little slower and will speak at 120–140 words per minute, whereas a Northerner will speak at approximately 140–160 words per minute. If we are listening at over 400 words per minute, where do our minds wonder while the person is speaking? We mentally write our grocery lists, decide on what to have for dinner, etc. So, to keep our listener's "tuned-in" and interested, we have to vary our speech pattern and be enthusiastic and energetic when on the phone.

If you want to build rapport with your telephone comrade, then use their name early and often in the conversation. People love to hear their name! My precaution here, however, is to use the formal name until you are invited to use the informal name. For instance, at first contact you should refer to someone as "Ms. Smith" rather than "Sally." Once they invite you to use their informal name, you can do so. Until that invitation, continue to use the formal name.

This may sound trite, but BEFORE you pick up the phone, SMILE. Really! Smile! People can see and hear your smile over the phone. It's easy to send a positive message through your voice when you are smiling. Smiling reduces the chance of sounding irritated, improves pronunciation, and voice tone, and increases the chance of a friendly conversation. Finally, it's hard to say, "you're a smuck" when you are smiling!

Answer a business call by the second ring. Your company probably has specific requirements on how they prefer you to answer the call. It is always appropriate to identify your company and yourself immediately. Use a greeting when you answer the phone. "Good morning, ABC Company. This is Jana. May I help you?" It starts the conversation on a positive, friendly, and professional note.

Speak directly into the mouthpiece and speak slowly and clearly. Never, never, never answer the phone while chewing gum or food. Your chewing will be heard and your words will be muffled! Eliminate loud background noise, which includes typing, carrying on numerous conversations or shuffling papers while talking to someone. They can hear it! The message this sends is simple: You are not important enough to have my full attention.

Call Waiting and Holding

Asking someone to hold should be the exception rather than the rule. Call waiting can be a wonderful tool, but can be the source of irritation and resentment in a business environment. It is really annoying when one is talking and all of the sudden, the infamous "bleep" cuts in and several words (and thoughts) are lost.

> **"Call waiting should be called "Call Rude." To put someone on hold to see if you've gotta better deal on the other line is downright rude!"**
>
> **—Gary Gabbard, CPC**

Recently, I answered the telephone and the caller jumped into a full-blown conversation, without asking me if I had a minute and began asking me to do give a free speech for her organization. During her rambling, her call waiting continued to click in. She would interrupt herself, say, "Oh, I need to answer that. Just a minute." She not only didn't ask if this was a good time for ME for a conversation, she didn't wait for my reply when her call waiting interrupted. The third time this happened in a span of 2–3 minutes, I told her to call me back at a more convenient time. I turned down the invitation to do the speech, by the way. The impression she gave me was not one of professionalism and I was concerned with the way the speaking engagement would be handled. I do very limited free speaking and I am very selective in the organizations I donate my time to as I speak for a living.

It's imperative, however, that you are polite if someone asks you to hold. If you do not have time, simply say, "I am sorry, but I don't have the time to hold right now. Would you mind calling back at a time when we will not be interrupted?"

Are you aware that most telephone companies provide the feature of allowing you to block call waiting? Check with your telephone company to see what the code is to block call waiting. Normally, you will press * (star) and two digits.

In all "holding" situations, you need to always:

1. Ask the caller BEFORE placing them on hold if it is okay.
2. Thank the caller before placing them on hold.
3. Keep your caller informed. If you need to look up information, tell them what you are doing. Don't leave them holding a dead phone with no clue as to whether you are still with them. When it is necessary, explain why and break in periodically to let the caller know they haven't been forgotten.
4. Thank the caller AGAIN when you come back on the line to continue the conversation.

Remember that people hate to be put on hold. If what you are doing will take longer than a few minutes, ask if you can call back. Write down your commitment to call back and don't miss it. Your word is your bond.

Caller ID

I was shocked! I recently taught a social manners class of 43 students between the ages of 10 and 14 years old at Southern Methodist University. When I asked the question how many of them had Caller ID at home, 90% raised their hands!

Caller ID seems to have taken quite a hold in the telephone industry. It is a great device in screening calls. Finally, a technology device has been invented to screen out those unwanted calls. Of course, I have noticed that most calls come in as "unavailable" or "private" (which means they have blocked Caller ID) or "outside the area." Oh-oh, I am caught! Yes, I have Caller ID and I admit it! I love it. For me, Caller ID is a definite telephone improvement. However, again, with this new technology device, come new rules.

Let's consider this scenario: We call a friend. We are in the process of leaving a message. Suddenly, the person we are leaving the message for interrupts us. They answer the phone, pretending to be out of breath and say, "Oh, Janie! I just came in from the garden. How are you?" Does she really expect us to believe that she was not sitting there listening to our message all along!??

With Caller ID, this scenario can be eliminated. We no longer have to screen our calls by listening to our answering machines and after a few sentences, say those UNBELIEVABLE words again!

Caller ID is a wonderful device to help us screen out the telemarketers who only call during dinner. The telemarketing world has gotten a lot more clever, however, with now having actual names showing up on the Caller ID box instead of "out of area," "anonymous" and other such messages.

It is most important when using Caller ID, that we don't pick up the phone and yell, "Hey, Jason!! How's it going!!??" It remains the polite thing to do, to answer with a friendly, "Hello."

Who's Calling, Please?

This has always been a touchy issue. The rule of etiquette is simple, however. Check the availability of a person BEFORE asking the caller's name. If you ask the caller's name and THEN say they are not in or on another line, the message is clear to the caller . . . they aren't available to YOU!

Too Much Information

I used to work in a law office and was constantly amazed at the receptionist's explanations as to why an attorney wasn't able to take a call. Among one of her responses when asked for an attorney, she said, "Oh, George (not the real name), isn't available right now. He just took a crossword puzzle into the bathroom and when he takes his crossword in there, he is there for ages!" This is a TRUE story!

One of her other responses floored me as well. "I'm sorry. Sam (not the real name) isn't in right now. He had to go downtown to see his attorney. He is filing for divorce today." Sam's area of specialization . . . a divorce attorney! What message did that send to the caller????

It's much better to use phrases such as, 'Joe isn't available at the moment." 'Joe stepped away from his desk." 'Joe is out of the office today." 'Joe is in a meeting." "She's not in her office at the moment."

Transferring the Caller

First and foremost, avoid the word "transfer." Use words or phrases like "connect," "talk with," "speak with," and "put in touch with." These are stronger words that carry a positive message rather than the old word, "transfer" which immediately sends a negative message. If necessary, explain why you have to connect them with someone else. Make sure someone is there before completing the transfer. If possible, tell the person to whom you are transferring the call, the caller's name and nature of the call.

When a Call Is Disconnected

The person who placed the call should initiate the call to reconnect, no matter whose phone was responsible for the lost connection.

Hold, Please!

People hate to be put on hold. In many of my seminars, I ask the participants to put their heads down, close their eyes and think of their favorite place to go on a vacation. I give them a few seconds to do this. I then ask them to raise their hand when they think one minute is up. I have seen the results of this exercise change over the years that I have been training. Several years ago, many participants would not raise their hand until about 45–50 seconds passed. Today, every time, every hand will be up by the time 30 seconds (maximum) has passed. We are such an impatient society. With this in mind, when you are the person asking the caller to hold, it is important to realize the global disease of "Impatience." Use hold carefully.

First and foremost, ask the caller if you may put them on hold and WAIT for their answer. I've experienced it . . . you've experienced it . . . the person who answers the phone, "ABC Corporation. Hold, please!" (Well, sometimes, they will say "please.") Before you can even respond, you are listening to music that you used to listen to ONLY in your parent's car when you were growing up. Oh, the memories come flooding back! Here are a few courtesy rules when putting someone on the dreaded "hold."

- ☎ Ask FIRST
- ☎ WAIT for the RESPONSE
- ☎ Tell them WHY they are being put on hold. This can be as simple as saying, "Mr. Jones is on the other line right now. Would you like to hold or would you prefer to leave him a message?" Never promise the caller that you will have Mr. Jones return the call. You do not have control

over whether or not Mr. Jones returns his call. Simply offer to take a message. The rest is up to Mr. Jones.

- Give estimates of the time you expect the caller to hold. If the hold time becomes longer than expected, offer to call them back. Write down your commitment and don't miss it.
- Thank the caller BEFORE and AFTER they are put on hold. This does not mean that you should say, "I'm sorry you had to hold." Do not apologize if it was their option to hold. Simply say a polite "thank you" for them holding.
- Check the availability of the person before asking the caller's name and putting them on hold. Often when I have been placed on hold for untold minutes, the person who put me on hold will come back on the line and say, "Mr. Smith isn't available." The message to me is very clear . . . He isn't available to ME! He just doesn't want to take my call. Even if that is not the case, that is the message that is sent.
- Most of all, it is very important that when you are putting a caller on hold that you keep them "tuned-in." Keep them informed of the estimated hold time. Never put a caller on hold and forget them. This leaves a terrible impression of you and your company. Periodically, break in to let the caller know she hasn't been forgotten.

Taking a Message

As previously discussed, with almost everyone having a voice mail system of some sort, we rarely have a message taken by a real human. However, there are a few general rules of courtesy that need to be observed when taking a message for a co-worker or family member:

- Explain your co-worker/family member's absence in a positive light. A simple "He's not available right now" is all that is necessary.
- Offer to help the caller yourself. If you cannot help the caller, then continue to take a message.
- Be sure to get the correct spelling and number, with area code of the caller's name.
- Repeat the name and number to them.
- If the caller says, "Oh, Zelda knows my number!" Simply respond with, "I understand she probably does, however, she has asked me to ALWAYS get the number." Or you could say something such as, "I understand she probably does, however, she will be calling you from the road and may not have it with her."
- Offer to take a BRIEF message. If your caller starts going into great detail, as soon as they take a breath, this is the time to restate what you have heard in a "bulleted" or "summary" response.

- ☎ Be sure to write down the date and time of the call. This can be beneficial to you and the person the message is for.
- ☎ Write down all important information.

Playing Telephone Tag or Exchanging Pink Slips

You've said it yourself! "Tag! You're it!" It can become very frustrating after several times of leaving messages to try to reach someone and they return your calls, only NOW you aren't there to receive it. This happens a lot in our office as we are out so often on the road conducting training. I have made it a habit that after the first time of leaving a message to say, "I will be at this number at this time. If for some reason you get my voice mail again, please leave me the best time to return your call." This has cut through the voice mail jail tête-à-tête many times.

Dealing With Chatty Cathy

Let's face it . . . some callers just want to talk and talk and talk and talk without regard for your schedule. I, perhaps, have even been accused of this myself . . . never to my face, of course. <grin>

How do we defuse the chatty caller? Before you defuse or dismiss, it is important to evaluate the real purpose of the call. Some of my business clients love to talk and these calls can take a long time. Since they are paying the bills, so to speak, I let them talk. When friends and family call and want to tell me the same stories that I heard at Thanksgiving in 1976, 1977, 1978, 1979 . . . well, you get the picture, I want to scream. As I get older (more mature) I am afraid that I, too, am starting to repeat the same story over and over. I think my children would like to make a comment here, but I am not going to let them. They can write their own book someday.

Here are the techniques I use to prevent or break in to long-winded stories. Keep in mind, this is polite!

- ☎ I don't ask questions. It's only logical that the chatty person is hoping for this and they not only answer your questions, they just keep going with a new subject title. You have just given them the ammunition they needed to continue chatting.
- ☎ Have you ever asked a hypochondriac how they feel? Oh, my goodness! They will tell you all of their ailments from the time they were born. The worse thing with this type of person is while they are talking, they come up with new, exciting and improved ailments to discuss with you! We now have not only the ill person, but they have become very knowledgeable in all areas of remedies. It's amazing how people are able to obtain an M.D. after their name by

just having the problem. So, bottom line, don't ask the chatty person how they feel.

- Don't offer information or comments. If you do, this opens the door for their "view" of the comments and information.
- Don't counter their story, situation or scenario with a like one of your own. Ninety-five percent of us listen autobiographically anyway and since we have a tendency to listen this way, it's very hard not to counter with our own story. Sometimes it can appear as a "one upsmanship" response anyway. My husband and I travel to Hawaii 2–3 times a year. We know the islands very well and especially Kauai, which is our favorite. When other people start telling us about their one-time experience in Hawaii, I have to really concentrate on what I say (or don't say) so that I do not appear to be up-staging them. It's best to agree, say nothing, or ooh and ah a lot. Actually, I love hearing any stories from people about their Hawaiian experiences.
- Again, if you start responding with your own stories, the conversation can never come to an end and the Chatty Cathy just keeps on going!
- THE GREAT ESCAPE—Here is the best technique for being polite while bringing the conversation to a close. When Chatty Cathy takes

a breath (and at some point, she will), immediately begin talking yourself with a simple comment, like, "Oh, Cathy, that is very interesting. I have never had that experience personally, but it sounds fascinating and I would love to be able to talk with you longer, but I am expected in a meeting in just a few minutes and need to go. Please take care and we'll talk again soon. Good bye." Whatever you do, don't breath and let her comment back. Conclude the conversation convincingly with finality in your voice.

Handling an Irate Caller

This can be difficult and a few people have told me that they just hang up on them. That is a possible solution, however, if we are in the customer service industry and the irate caller is a customer, we don't have that luxury. Besides, it is our job to know how to handle the irate customer.

It's important to recognize our own behavior when we are angry or respond to an angry person. Know your signals. What do you do when you are angry or stressed? I can tell you that I lock my jaw, grit my teeth and squint my eyes. Once you recognize what your angry signals are, do the opposite. Unlock that jaw, take deep breaths, and open your eyes. We have to remain in control if we are going to adequately handle the caller, right?

- Let the caller vent. When you have an irate caller, they are emotionally psycho! Let them vent their feelings.
- Don't interrupt. Have you ever been so angry that you practiced what you are going to say? You may prepare a bulleted list in your head or know the issues you are going to address from A to Z. If you interrupt the caller when they are on "P," they will automatically go back to "A" when they regain the floor.
- Try to analyze what the real problem is. Many times when irate people are venting, they go off of the main anger point to "sub-points" that they really don't care about, but they like to throw more fuel on the fire.
- Use the caller's name. There is something about hearing your name that helps to calm you down.
- Restate. This is one of the most effective ways to defuse an angry person. Listen to what they are saying very carefully. Once they have told you their problem, from A to Z, restate what you believe to be the real problem, which may only be C and D. This technique will do two things. One, if you get it right, they will agree. Two, if you get it wrong, they will tell you the real issue, which may be J and K.
- Avoid emotional "trigger" words. Remember that "Courtesy is Charisma." Don't use words

like "company policy, you should have, calm down, but, the only thing I can do, can't, no, can't help you, you have to."

- Use positive words. Use words such as, "Here's what I can do for you, yes, can, thank you, I can find out, I understand why you . . . ." Remember to be soothing and to use extremely courteous words that will calm the emotionally challenged.
- Use friendly, tactful language. Never accuse and never convey that your caller's request is an imposition.
- Show empathy. Handle irate callers with understanding and care. Use techniques such as asking for desired solutions and agreeing upon a solution.
- If the caller is abusive, use help statements. "Ms. Zipperfoot, (using the name) I would like to help you (help statement), however (don't use the weak word, "but") I find it difficult when you are [yelling] [using this kind of language]. Will you let me help you?"
- Thank the caller for calling even when they are angry. Remember that we learn from our mistakes and problems more than from our success. View the complaint as an opportunity to be better.
- Let the caller hang up first so that she doesn't accidentally get cut off in the middle of a sentence.

No matter how "high-tech" we have become, when dealing with an irate caller, we must remember to be "high-touch" and understanding. Think about your image every time you are on the phone.

> **"You have only one opportunity to make a dynamic first impression in all aspects of image."**
>
> —JODIE WALLACE, INSPIRING IMAGES

Chapter 11

Voice Mail

Putting Your Best Voice Forward

A customer sent their lease car payment to the wrong address. When the payment was late, the car leasing company called the customer. The customer answered the phone to a customer service representative who asked, "Is this Mr. Smith?" When the customer said yes, he was then instructed to hold for an important recorded message. Mr. Smith listened for a few minutes and the recording said that his payment had not been received and asked when he was going to send it. Mr. Smith didn't feel like having a conversation with a machine, so he hung up.

A week or so later, another call, same routine . . . This time, determined not to be trapped in a one-sided conversation, he said that he didn't want to talk to a machine. There was silence while the service agent regrouped. She then continued, "You HAVE to listen to the recording!" Mr. Smith refused again. The customer service representative retorted, "If you don't listen to the recording, you are going to have to talk to a real person!"

You can see from this true scenario why there are advocates and adversaries of voice mail. The advocates say it saves time. Callers can leave detailed information so the recipient can act before returning the call. It is more accurate than personal message taking, you don't have to waste time "small talking" and a factor that I really like is that I can leave messages in the late night hours when I do my most efficient work.

The adversaries tell us that their callers object to talking to a machine. They are afraid it removes the personal touch. In business, many companies are now advertising better, personalized service, and they have "real people" answering the phones. Another problem that adversaries point out is that people don't return their voice mail messages promptly.

Used properly, voice mail can increase productivity by using it when you are out of your office or in a conference. It helps to let you focus on the customer or person you are with without interruptions.

Using proper telephone etiquette will help whether recording or leaving a message. Following are some basic ideas for recording the message your callers will hear.

Basics of Recording Your Voice Mail Message

A friend of mine wrote the following story to me as she thought I would get a laugh out of it. "A friend of ours was puzzled with the odd messages left on his answering machine. Day after day friends and family would talk and then say, "Beep."

He discovered the reason for the joke when he decided to listen to his greeting. "Hi," it said, "I'm not in right now, so please leave a beep after the message."

My friend was right! I loved this story!

This story shows the reason why we should always practice our recordings before we start. I even write mine down and practice it before I press record.

> **"Before recording your message, practice it. Your voice inflection along with your language is important. These concepts create a definite image when the caller listens to your message."**
>
> —JODIE WALLACE, INSPIRING IMAGES

Make Your Message Valuable

Don't waste time recording lame excuses of *why* you are not answering your phone. Don't say, "I'm away from my desk, I'm on the other line, I'm with another valuable customer, I'm not available right now" or any other of those canned phrases! It's obvious that you aren't around or you would have answered your phone!

No Overtures, Please!

Not only am I extremely irritated by the "overture" before the recorded message, so are many others. I have heard this complaint over and over in many of my seminars. Several people have said that as soon as they hear the music, they hang up!

"People who leave long greetings are truly annoying. 'Hi! This is Buddy Boy, your call is very important to me. I am away from my desk or on the other line. Would you please leave your full name and spell your last name slowly, your telephone number, and please repeat it twice, along with a detailed purpose of your call. I will return your call as quickly as possible. Our rates today on five year fixed annuities is ....' and on and on and on!"

—PETER KRAUSE, THE INSURANCE HOUSE

Make Your Message Specific

You can either say, "Thank you for calling the High's" (my family name) or if it is a business line, "Thank you for calling JLH Presentations." This identifies that the caller has reached the number they intended to dial.

"One of my pet peeves with recorded messages are the ones that tell their business hours and other time consuming "stuff" before you can dial an extension or leave a message. After business hours, it's great to hear a message saying they are closed. 'Our hours are 9–5 Monday through Friday. Please leave a message.'"

—ROBERT DRAPEAU, PERIMETER EXHIBITS, LTD.

Make It Timely

I change my recording at the office at least once a month. Often, if I am going to be away from the office for an extended period of time, I will ask the caller to leave a "best time" for me to return their call or I will leave an optional number where I can be reached if their call is urgent. Change the message when it is appropriate to do so.

> **"It is very unprofessional when people don't change their voice mail message when they are going to be out of the office or unavailable for an extended amount of time. If I leave a voice mail message, then I expect a call back within 24 hours. It's always been my policy to return calls the same business day I receive them. If I am going to be out of the office for any reason (vacation, surgery, conference, etc) then I feel it is my professional responsibility to inform my callers of my extended absence and offer them another number they may call for immediate attention. It's just good business practice!"**
>
> —F. Howard Manning, Parkway Bank

Make Your Recording Professional

Be professional when you are recording a message for a business. When it is for your home phone, keep it simple and to the point. I am amazed by some of the recorded messages that I have listened to from businesses that I am trying to reach. I have one friend who owns her own business and her recorded message goes something like this, "Thank you for calling XYZ Company. I am away from my desk, out of the office, or with another valuable customer and cannot talk to you right now. However, I want to 'light up your life' with our fabulous XYZ products, so please leave a message after you hear the beep. If this is a valuable customer and you want to place an order, that I greatly appreciate and promise to fill right away, please leave your entire order at the end of this message. If you are one of my district managers, please don't forget the weekly Saturday meeting at 9:00 a.m. that will be held at my house, located at 12345 South Street, which is on the corner of North and West. Now, wait for that beep to record your message. And be sure and have a super terrific day!"

YIKES!!!! As soon as her message starts, I hang up, especially if I am calling from my cell phone! This is just too much information and lacks professionalism, not to mention being irritating. No one wants to listen to all of this information. Many professional people use their cell phones for business and will be calling you and leaving messages. Remember to be brief and precise when you record your message.

Once again, remember the old saying, "Practice makes perfect." Practice before you record and strive for perfection!

Basics of Leaving a Voice Mail Message

Have you ever left a message on someone's recorder that as soon as you said what you said, you wanted to take it back? Many sitcoms, such as *Seinfeld*, *Frasier*, and *Friends*, have dedicated an entire show to the humorous side of the main characters leaving messages on peoples' voice mail machines. The scenario is always the same. They didn't think ahead of time as to what they were going to say and then they say something really stupid and want to take it back, but of course, it is too late.

So, my number one hint about leaving a méssage is simple . . . **HAVE NO REGRETS! BEFORE** you pick up the phone and start dialing, THINK about what you want to say. This brings me to my next point of leaving a message.

> **"If you have nothing to say, don't leave a voice mail. However, if you want a return call, leave your name and number and briefly state the purpose of your call."**
>
> **—Kelly Jackson, Card Payment Services**

Leave Your Name

And spelling helps. Even if you are a friend or frequent caller, don't expect your party to recognize your voice. Protocol dictates that you always leave your name, first AND last, at the beginning and the end of your message. To this day, my husband calls and says, "Jana, this is Lee." Now, there is one voice that I had better recognize, but he has been trained from youth to always state his name. I believe that it is important for parents to instill this practice in their children as soon as they are old enough to make calls or receive calls. Children, as well as adults, should know the proper manner of handling the phone. If they don't, they shouldn't be using it.

Always—Always Leave Your Telephone Number, with Area Code!

Say it at the beginning of your message and once again at the end. If you expect a call back, make this a habit. Many people travel today and retrieve their messages from a remote location. Few of us carry our entire address book with phone numbers with us. Again, even if you are a frequent caller or good friend, leave your number. Our heads are already bursting with numbers from our driver's license to our frequent flyer numbers. Make it easy to receive a call back.

Leave a Short Message

I have a very dear friend who leaves her message until the recorder cuts her off. She is not discouraged! Oh no, she calls back as many times as it takes to continue her message. If I am retrieving my messages using my cell phone or from a long distance number, I immediately hit "save" and wait to retrieve her message until I get back to the office. I am sure that this has resulted in not returning her messages within my 24-hour rule, but if I am on the road, I have no choice. Simply, leave the pertinent information and ask for a return call.

If Calling From a Cellular Phone

Be aware that your message may cut in and out or be garbled. Even though cell phones continue to improve, they are not perfect. I have had trouble periodically retrieving my messages from the office when using my cell phone and I just can't get the whole name, number, or message. This is another reason to repeat your name and number at the beginning and end of each message you leave.

Speak Slowly!

When you leave your number, pretend that you are writing it with the dashes and spaces. This will help you to speak at a pace that the retriever can write it down so that she may call you back. To this day, over and over, people still say their number so fast, that I have to hit "replay" several times. When I am calling long distance or from my cell phone, if I can't get the number with one "replay" I wait until I am in the office to retrieve and return the call.

"An unprofessional voice mail message that includes stuttering and stammering and is not thought out shows a lack of intelligence. Remember that your voice mail is your billboard advertisement of who you are."

—Henry Gentry, Henry's Homemade Ice Cream

These rules are really just common courtesy. Unfortunately, we are in such a hurry-up, fast paced world today, that we just don't slow down enough to take the time for simple considerations. Be prepared. Be precise. Get to the point and leave the important information if you expect a call back.

Chapter 12

Speakerphone Savvy and Conference Call Courtesy

After you! No, After YOU! NO, NO, After YOU!

"Nature has given men one tongue and two ears, that we may hear twice as much as we speak."

—EPICTETUS

Although I am not fond of speakerphones in general, they do serve a purpose. Almost everyone that I have interviewed about the use of speakerphones has adamantly said they despise them. I understand their feelings. One primary comment I heard over and over was the privacy issue. When being placed on a speakerphone, they didn't know who else was listening to their conversation.

Another comment that I received repeatedly is that they were not getting the person's full attention as they could hear papers rustling, staplers clinking, and keyboards clicking.

Speakerphones can be a useful tool if the people using them observe a few simple rules. The most important rule of etiquette is to ask permission before putting someone on the speakerphone. This should actually be prearranged if it is a conference call.

- Identify everyone in the room where the speakerphone is being used.
- In using a speakerphone or during a conference call, you should introduce yourself or have a leader that introduces everyone.

- When you begin to speak during a conference call, identify yourself and to whom you are addressing your question or comment.
- Use short sentences and ask simple questions.
- Don't dominate. I have sat in on conference calls where one person monopolized the entire conversation I didn't know why we were all on the line.

The final comment regarding speakerphones is what should you do when you have been put on speakerphone and have not been asked? Do you have the right to ask to be taken off of the speakerphone? The answer is yes, you have that right and honesty is the best policy. You have every right to ask the person to take you off the speakerphone. If you don't know the person well or you don't want to be blunt, you can simply say, "I am sorry. I am having trouble hearing you. Would you mind taking me off the speakerphone?" I used this technique several times and no one has objected to my request.

Chapter 13

Travelling with Electronic Equipment

The Vagabond, When Rich, Is Called a Tourist

All I really wanted to do was to read my magazine, have a typical mediocre airplane meal and relax. I knew that when I arrived in Atlanta that I would be so busy that I would have no "chill-out" time.

Then, the man beside me started to talk to the guy across the aisle in a loud, irritating voice. I could tell that he thought that everyone wanted to hear him, because we all needed to be impressed with his anecdotes. Finally, after being glared at by many fellow travelers, he shut up. But I noticed that he was restless. He was toe tapping, gum chewing, knuckle breaking and I knew that any moment he was going to explode. But no! Instead, he got into his briefcase and pulled out his laptop computer. I thought to myself that this was a good idea as maybe he would quiet down. Silly me! As he opened his computer and notebook, he proceeded to take up a seat and a half. (The other half was mine) He started typing fast and furious. All that was going through my mind was that old song that went "Yackety-Yak, Don't Come Back." It was then that I knew . . . there's no escape!

In 1949, three years after engineers built the first electronic computers, *Popular Mechanics Magazine* predicted that computers in the future might have only 1,000 tubes and weigh only one and a half tons. Today, a five pound laptop can process data faster than the largest mainframes at mid-century. Wow! Did we fool Popular Mechanic's prediction! There is more computing power in a greeting card today than existed in the 1950s!

Cellular telephones, laptops, PDAs, and beepers are all so much a part of our modern life that we take many of them for granted and don't remember a time we didn't have these small, lightweight conveniences. Modern technology provides us with constant access to every place in the world. Isn't it true that it is commonplace to see people talking on their wireless cell phones almost everywhere? They are carrying on conversations while driving their cars, walking down the street or shopping in the grocery store. Again, although these are wonderful conveniences, is it proper to conduct business or carry on personal conversations just anywhere? I believe that we are so used to the convenience of portable electronic communications today that many of us forget that when using these devices, we seem to have a lapse of concentration in exercising sensible manners.

Incredible breaches of the most common courtesies occur on airplanes and other traveling modes. We need to remember that we don't "own" our seat, but rather we "rent" it from the transportation company and all areas on planes, trains, and automobiles are "shared space."

Here are a few common courtesies to remember while traveling with electronic equipment.

- Remember when traveling that your space is considered to be from shoulder-to-shoulder. That is YOUR shoulder, not your neighbors!

- Watch your tap, tap, tap, click, click, click. This is especially true in libraries, classrooms or anyplace that is supposed to be quiet or where your noise may interfere with others' ability to concentrate.
- Use inside voices. Save your animated and loud conversations for private places.
- If you are going to use a piece of electronic equipment to play games, turn off the sound.
- When using a public telephone, don't perch. Be considerate of those around you that may want to place a call as well. Public phones are not your office space.
- Remember that electronic equipment will probably be subjected to extra security searches in airports and other places where items you carry are screened. At the very least, you will be asked to remove your laptop from its bag and place it on a separate tray for screening. Be prepared for this and don't delay the line while you search for the key to unlock the bag and then unpack the bag because you put the computer on the bottom. And don't be upset if you are asked to open your bag for a physical inspection because the security scan showed several items with batteries and wires and other suspicious components. Acting indignant or becoming angry will not speed up the process for you, or for the unfortunate ones in line behind you.

- Even though we now have armed military guards at airport security stations, thieves are still making off with purses, bags and laptop computers. Be alert and watch your belongings while you are going through the security process. Do not send your bags through the machine until you are ready to proceed through the metal detector yourself. Watch out for someone cutting in front of you and stalling at the metal detector. While you are delayed on the outside, someone else may be taking your computer and bags.
- In some airports you may be asked to turn on your computer or other electronic equipment to show that they are genuine. If you are asked to do this, make sure the battery is charged or have the power cord handy. Also, remember to turn them off afterwards. More than once I have seen people discover later that in the hurry to repack everything, they forgot to turn them off and now, when they want to use them, the batteries are dead.
- Airlines now restrict us to one carry on bag and one "personal" item, such as a purse, briefcase or computer bag. Please do not try to claim a second carry on bag as a computer bag. I sometimes travel with a load of equipment (computer, printer, projector, and all of the associated cables and power adaptors). Don't try and

stretch the airline's regulations, and the flight attendants' patience. Check a bag if you must.

- That empty middle seat is not really empty until the doors close on the plane. Don't spread your stuff out, hoping to discourage anyone from sitting there. That's plain rude in the waiting area but onboard the plane it is both rude and useless. If a passenger shows up at the last minute with a boarding pass for that seat, you will have to clean up your "office." I have seen passengers who loudly refused to remove their stuff from the seat, shouting that they were frequent fliers with super platinum status and the middle seat was supposed to be blocked for them. Guess who won the argument.
- In restaurants, don't claim squatter's rights to your table. Buying a cup of coffee doesn't entitle you to sit and read the Sunday New York Times. And a cup of coffee isn't rental on making the table your office. Other people may be waiting for a table and the waiter or waitress would probably like to earn more than your solitary tip for the day.

It only takes common consideration for others to make life more pleasant in public places. We all have to go through the same security procedures. We all have to wait in the same cramped areas. We all have to sit in the same narrow seats. Becoming upset or trying to take extra space doesn't solve the problem.

Several years ago my husband was departing from Moscow. The airport procedures in Moscow add new meaning to the request to "be at the airport two hours before flight time." First you join a large crowd trying to enter the Customs area through a single small gate, then in Customs you go through a complete inspection of every bag, then on to the ticket counter to check your bags and get a boarding pass, and finally to Passport Control. Patience and good humor are essential.

One day the man in front of my husband in the Customs line was objecting very loudly to having his bags searched. The Russian customs officer, wearing his best stone face look just continued to go through the bags very slowly and very carefully. Eventually he found something, which was pulled out and set aside.

The man was then passed through, now protesting all the more. He continued to voice his opinions all the way through the baggage check in and was pacing around the area between the airline desk and Passport Control, still outraged that his bags had been searched and something confiscated.

My husband was standing in line at Passport Control when the man calmed down and went to the front of the line. At that point, a militia officer, smiling broadly, came up and took him by the arm and escorted him to the rear of the line. The loud protests over this treatment started all over again. And to no avail.

Remember to be patient and to remain courteous. You and your fellow passengers will all feel better.

Chapter 14

When It's All Said and Done . . .

It's All About Common Sense Communication

Once upon a time, there were four people named EVERYBODY, SOMEBODY, NOBODY and ANYBODY.

When there was an important job to be done, EVERYBODY was sure that SOMEBODY would do it.

ANYBODY could have done it, but NOBODY did it.

When NOBODY did it, SOMEBODY got angry because it was EVERYBODY's job.

EVERYBODY thought that ANYBODY could do it, but NOBODY realized that SOMEBODY wouldn't do it.

So it ended up that EVERYBODY blamed SOMEBODY and NOBODY did what ANYBODY could have done in the first place.

So, when all is said and done, it's all about communication skills in a high tech world. We cannot ignore communication protocol. We must be considerate, professional, and courteous.

We are responsible for what we say and what we write, whether to our Aunt Zelda or to the CEO of a major corporation.

High-Tech communication will never replace the thrill of finding a sweet note from an old friend, a small little gift that fits in a square envelope, or some silly old photographs in your mailbox, but it does serve a purpose.

We can enjoy all media of communication if we just remember the rules of protocol and common courtesy and never forget that our first impression is our lasting impression. Make yours great!

Appendix 1

Emoticons

The Smiley Face ☺ and Some Basic Variations

:-)	Basic Smiley
:)	Basic Smiley without Nose (Note—Noses are optional for all of the Smileys. We'll just show the versions with noses.)
(-:	Left Handed Smiley
:^)	Profile Smiley
;-)	Winking
:-, ;^)	Smirk
:->	Sarcastic
;->	Devilish Wink, Tongue-in-Cheek
:-y	Said With a Smile
:-(:-<	Sad
:-c	Very Sad
:-C	Very, Very Sad
:'-(	Crying
:'-)	So Happy I'm Crying
:-*	Kissing (also Oops)
:-X	Big Kiss
:-x	Little Kiss, Kiss Kiss

:-{ }	Blowing a Kiss
:0) :)	Clown-Face
;-(	Disappointed
>:-||	Angry
>:-(	Very Angry
>:-<	Livid
:-]	Jovial or Smiling Blockhead
:-[	Pouty, Despondent or Un-smiling Blockhead
:-o	Surprised
:-O	Shocked (also Yelling or "oops")
=:-O	Scared
8-|	Eyes Wide with Surprise
8-O	Omigod!
:-0	Yelling
:-@	Screaming
:-V	Shouting
:-/	Skeptical, Confused or Undecided
:~/	Mixed Up
/:-(	Worried
:-D	Laughing
O:-)	Angelic

<table>
<tr><td>}:-)</td><td>Devilish</td></tr>
<tr><td>:-I</td><td>Indifferent</td></tr>
<tr><td>:-|</td><td>Grim</td></tr>
<tr><td>:-Q</td><td>Confused</td></tr>
<tr><td>\-o</td><td>Bored</td></tr>
<tr><td>|-O</td><td>Yawning</td></tr>
<tr><td>|-I</td><td>Sleepy</td></tr>
<tr><td>!-(</td><td>Black Eye</td></tr>
<tr><td>:-&</td><td>Tongue-Tied</td></tr>
<tr><td>:-S</td><td>Incoherent</td></tr>
<tr><td>:-"</td><td>Pursed Lips</td></tr>
<tr><td>:-X :-#</td><td>Sealed Lips</td></tr>
<tr><td>:-T</td><td>Straight Face or Tight Lipped</td></tr>
<tr><td>:-r</td><td>Sticking Tongue Out</td></tr>
<tr><td>:-P</td><td>Raspberry or Tongue Hanging Out in Anticipation</td></tr>
<tr><td>:-W</td><td>Lying (Speaking with a Forked Tongue)</td></tr>
<tr><td>:-Y</td><td>Quiet Aside, Speaking Out of the Side of Your Mouth</td></tr>
<tr><td>:-( )</td><td>Big Mouth, Non Stop Talker</td></tr>
<tr><td>:-6</td><td>Exhausted</td></tr>
<tr><td>:-9</td><td>Licking Lips or Yum</td></tr>
</table>

:-$	Put Your Money Where Your Mouth Is
# -) % -)	Big Night Last Night or Brain Dead
:-[	Vampire (also Pouty or Un-Smiling Block-head)
:-]	Happy Vampire
:-E	Vampire with Buck Teeth
:-F	Vampire with Broken Fang
8-# X-(	Dead

Celebrities, People and Animal Smileys

=|:-)=	Uncle Sam, Abraham Lincoln
8(:-)	Mickey Mouse
:-.)	Cindy Crawford, Marilyn Monroe
5:-J 5:O @:)	Elvis
:)B	Dolly Parton
<|:^)>>>	Santa Claus
+-<:-)	The Pope
%-~	Picasso
3:*>	Rudolph the Red Nosed Reindeer
:$)	Donald Trump
C|:-=	Charlie Chaplin

:———}	Pinocchio
@@@@8^)	Marge Simpson
=(_8^(1)	Homer Simpson
38^)	Bart Simpson
:-%	A Banker
:-:	A Mutant
(-:|:-)	Siamese Twins
C):-O C):-O C):-O C):-O	A Barbershop Quartet
3:-o	A Cow
8:-)	A Pig
><:->==	A Turkey
><:->==O	A Butterball Turkey
(:-I	Egghead
=:-)	Hosehead or Punk
<:-I	Dunce
[:]	Robot
>>:-)	Klingon
O-)	Cyclops

Smileys Describing Physical Characteristics	
&:-)	Curly Hair
#:-)	Bad Hair Day
(:-)	Bald or Wearing Bike Helmet
(-)	Needs a Haircut
d:-) p:-)	Baseball Cap
K:-)	Propeller Beanie
[:-)	Wearing a Walkman
B-)	Wearing Glasses
R-)	Broken Glasses
8-)	Sunglasses
8:-)	Sunglasses on Top of Head
:-#	Wearing Braces
{(:-) }(:-)	Toupee/Windy Day
:-)=	Beard
:-)>	Goatee
:0) :+)	Big Nose
:-~)	Runny Nose or Has a Cold
:-})	Moustache
{:-{)	Moustache and a Toupee

:-{}	Wearing Lipstick
@:-)	Wearing a Turban

Non-Smiley Emoticons

^5	High Five
^	Thumbs Up
(::()::)	Band-aid for Help or Support
[ ]	Hugs
{[( )]}	Group Hug
(( )):*:-)	Hugs and Kisses
][	Feeling Separate
] [	Moving Apart
) (	Really Far Apart
}{	Face to Face
\~/	Half-Full Glass (also sometimes Full Glass)
_/	Empty glass
@>–>—	A Rose
@}-'-,-'-,—	A Rose with Thorns
|*-*|	Cassette Tape
<*}}}>	Dead Fish

Appendix 2

Shorthand Expressions

Shorthand Expressions	
AAMOF	As A Matter Of Fact
AYPI?	And Your Point Is?
BFN	Bye For Now
BBFN	Bye Bye For Now
BRB	Be Right Back
BTDT	Been There Done That
BTW	By The Way
BYKT	But You Knew That
CMIIW	Correct Me If I'm Wrong
EOL	End Of Lecture, End Of Line
FAQ	Frequently Asked Questions
FITB	Fill In The Blank
FWIW	For What It's Worth
FYI	For Your Information
GG	Got to Go
HTH	Hope This Helps
IAC	In Any Case
IAE	In Any Event
ICL	In Christian Love
IMCO	In My Considered Opinion

IMHO	In My Humble Opinion
IMNSHO	In My Not So Humble Opinion
IMO	In My Opinion
IOW	In Other Words
KIT	Keep In Touch
L8R G8R	Later Gator
LOL	Laughing Out Loud or Lots Of Luck
LTNS	Long Time No See
MGB	May God Bless
MHOTY	My Hat's Off To You
NRN	No Reply Necessary
OIC	Oh, I See
OTOH	On The Other Hand
OTTOMH	Off The Top Of My Head
PM	Private Message
QSL	Reply
ROF	Rolling On the Floor
ROFL	Rolling On the Floor Laughing
ROTFL	Rolling On The Floor Laughing
RSN	Real Soon Now
SITD	Still In The Dark

SNAFU	Situation Normal, All Fouled Up
SPAM	Stupid Persons' Advertisement
TIC	Tongue In Cheek
TIA	Thanks In Advance
TTFN	Ta Ta For Now
TTYL	Talk To You Later
TYVM	Thank You Very Much
WYSIWYG	What You See Is What You Get
<G>	Grinning
<J>	Joking
<L>	Laughing
<S>	Smiling
<Y>	Yawning

Appendix 3

Shorthand Expressions

Teen Talk

Shorthand Expressions—Teen Talk	
ATM	At The Moment
AYT	Are You There?
BBL	Be Back Later
CYA	See You
DDG	Drop Dead Gorgeous
EOD	End Of Day
GTG	Got To Go
G8	Great
IGU	I Give Up
IMO	In My Opinion
JAM	Just A Minute
JC	Just Chilling
JIT	Just In Time
JJ	Just Joking
NE	Any
OIC	Oh, I See
POS	Parents Over Shoulder
RU	Are You
RUOK?	Are You Okay?
SUP	What's Up?

TOM	Tomorrow
(((hug)))	A Hug

Emoticons and Shorthand Expressions from:

www.pb.org/emoticon.html

www.windweaver.com/emoticon.html

www.chirpingbird.com/netpets/html/computer/emoticon.html

www.randonhouse.com/features/davebarry/emoticon.html

www.angelfire.com/hahakiam/emoticon.html

www.xs4all.nl/~ernstmul/emoticon.html

www.utopiasw.demon.co.uk/emoticon.html

www.ultranet.com/support/netiquette/emoticons.shtml

www.won.nl/dsp/usr/mvketel/Internet/emoticon.html

Dallas Morning News 11/28/2001, p. C1

Appendix 4

General E-Mail and Internet Information

What's in a Name—a Guide to Domain Names

Domain names are the part of the e-mail address that comes after the "at sign" (@) or after the "www." in the Internet address. For example, the address of this book is www.HighTechEtiquette.net. Thus, the domain name is "HighTechEtiquette.net." Domain names are a sort of shorthand address of the computers used to send and receive e-mail and Internet messages.

Initially computers identified other computers by a string of numbers. These numbers consist of ten digits, composed of four sets of numbers between 0–255 with each set separated by dots. Not only is that confusing, it is also nearly impossible to memorize or even type without making mistakes. This problem was solved in 1984 when the Domain Name System was developed. Computers still use the confusing string of numbers to talk to each other but we use more easily understood domain names.

The different parts of the domain name are separated by periods and refer to different levels of the organization, increasing in size from left to right. Most domain names consist of two parts, separated by a dot (.). The first part (in this case "HighTechEtiquette") identifies the local organization that is sending or receiving the message. Most organizations will only have a single level. Examples are "aa.com" for American Airlines, "barnesandnoble.com" for Barnes and

Noble and "irs.gov" for the friendly folks at the Internal Revenue Service. Larger organizations, especially governments and universities, may have several levels in their domain name and the left hand side of the name will then have two or more parts, also separated by dots. Examples are "gsbpop.uchicago.edu" for the Graduate School of Business at the University of Chicago and "arc.nasa.gov" for the Ames Research Center of the National Aeronautical and Space Administration.

At times, you may receive an e-mail with part of the domain name missing. This can occur if the person sending you the message has the same domain name as you do. For example, if jane@aol.com sends an e-mail to joe@aol.com then the message may show only "jane" as the return address.

The final part of the domain name is either two or three letters. These are the Top-Level Domains (TLDs). Two-letter TLDs refer to the country and three-letter TLDs refer to the type of organization. Originally, three-letter TLDs were used only in the US. Now, they may be used internationally, but most still refer to US organizations.

There are a limited number of three-letter TLDs that may be used. These are:

TLD	Organization
.com	commercial enterprise, business, company
.net	network provider, Internet Service Provider (ISP)
.gov	U.S. government
.edu	U.S. colleges and universities
.org	non-profit organization
.mil	U.S. military
.int	international

Recently, in response to the explosive growth of the internet, seven new TLDs have been approved for use. These new TLDs are more descriptive of the type of organization.

TLD	Organization
.info	unrestricted use
.biz	trademarked business names, general businesses

.name	personal names
.pro	professionals in specific areas such as law, medicine, accounting
.museum	museums and related professions
.aero	air transport industry
.coop	business cooperatives

Two-letter TLDs are abbreviations of the country name. The rules of usage vary from country to country. Most countries restrict usage to their citizens or organizations located within the country. The United States restricts the use of .us to governmental agencies, state and local governmental agencies, local schools, community colleges, museums, libraries, etc. The countries of Cocos and Tuvalu have sold their rights to their TLDs and anyone can register a domain name using .cc or .tv. Examples of country TLDs are:

TLD	Organization
.us	United States
.uk	United Kingdom
.de	Germany (Deutschland)
.jp	Japan

.nl	Netherlands
.ca	Canada
.ru	Russia
.tv	Tuvalu
.cc	Cocos (Keeling Islands)

A complete list of country codes can be found at: www.ics.uci.edu/pub/websoft/wwwstat/country-codes.txt

About the Author

Jana L. High is the president of JLH Presentations. She is an author as well as a full-of-energy seminar leader and keynote speaker. Jana's presentations are delivered with an enthusiastic and dynamic speaking style. Coupled with her ability to teach "usable" techniques for problem solving, Jana simply captivates her audiences.

Jana High is a specialist in communications, as well as fields of individual and career development. She is the founder of an established business education firm serving individuals, organizations and corporations nationwide. Her experience of living overseas and traveling extensively has broadened her ability to relate to individuals of all cultures and traditions.

In addition to serving as an Adjunct Instructor at Southern Methodist University, Jana has designed management and individual programs for industry leaders nationwide. Each presentation is customized for the industry she addresses.

Jana is available for seminars, corporate training and keynote presentations to groups of all sizes.

Seminar/Training topics include:

- High-Tech Etiquette
- Protocol for the Professional—Polishing Your Professional Presence to Perfection
- International Etiquette—Global Guidelines
- "Pardon Me! Is That Broccoli in Your Teeth?"—A Dining Decorum Seminar
- How to Develop the "WOW" in Customer Service—Developing Exceptional Customer Service

- Communicating with Confidence/PHD Networking—Powerful, Highly Effective, Dynamic Networking Skills
- The Magnificent Assistant—Skills for Administrative Assistants
- A Mission in Time and Space—Skills for Effective Time Management
- Stress Management
- Excelling in a Time of Change
- Teamwork
- Speak Up and Actually Be Heard
- The Master Manager—Moving from Manager to Leader
- How to Knock Their Socks Off and Keep Them Coming Back for More—A Customer Retention Program that Works

Keynotes:

- "Celebration"
- "The Princess Principle"
- "Life Dealt Me a Lemon"
- "The Gift"
- "Going the Distance"
- "Fortunately . . . Life's a Cookie!"

For further information or to schedule an event, please contact Jana at:

Jana L. High
JLH Presentations
3020 Legacy Drive, Suite 100-310
Plano, TX 75023
Phone: (972) 509-9171
Toll Free: (866) 820-6303
Fax: (972) 516-1510
jana@jlhpresentations.com
www.jlhpresentations.com